OVERVIEW BIBLE STU

FINDING YOUR WAY

A 50 LESSON JOURNEY THROUGH THE STORYLINE OF THE BIBLE

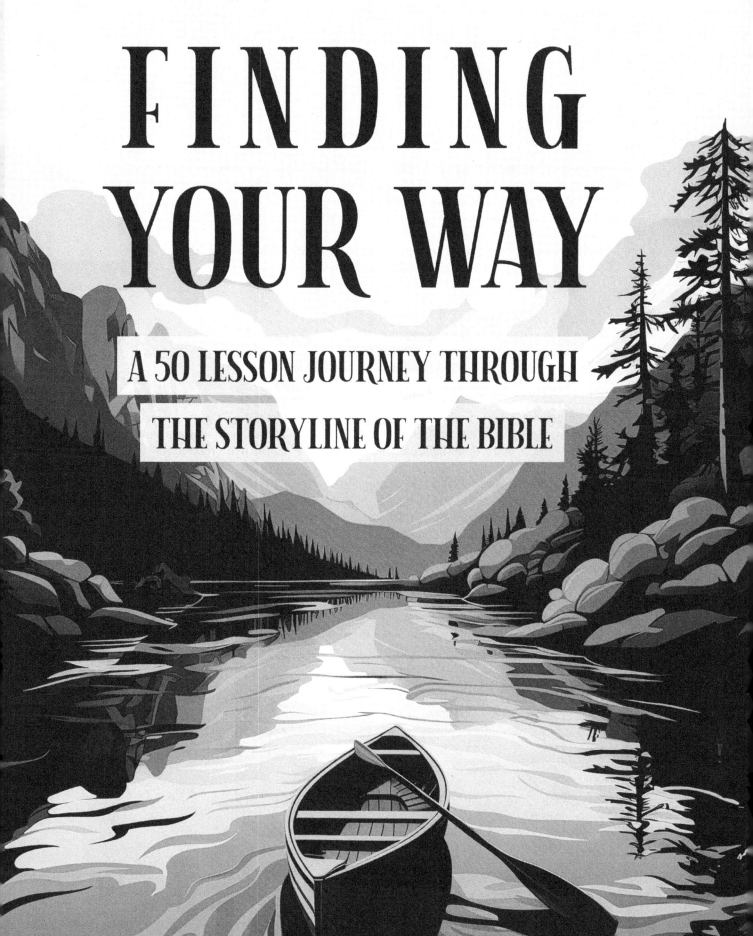

Copyright © 2023 Kimberly B. Burch

All rights reserved. No part of this work may be reproduced or transmitted in any form or by any means, electronic or mechanical, including photocopying and recording, or by any information storage or retrieval system, except as may be expressly permitted in writing by the author. Requests for permission should be addressed to the author at kim@visitccc.com.

Supplemental information and resources can be found at findingyourwaybiblestudy.com.
Email us at findingyourwaybiblestudy@gmail.com.

ISBN: 9798851195211

Interior Design by Elayna Macurak
Cover Design by Katarina Naskovski

Unless otherwise indicated, all Scripture quotations are taken from the Holy Bible, New Living Translation, copyright © 1996, 2004, 2015 by Tyndale House Foundation. Used by permission of Tyndale House Publishers, Carol Stream, Illinois 60188. All rights reserved.

Scripture quotations marked (NIV) are taken from the Holy Bible, New International Version®, NIV®. Copyright © 1973, 1978, 1984, 2011 by Biblica, Inc.™ Used by permission of Zondervan. All rights reserved worldwide. www.zondervan.com. The "NIV" and "New International Version" are trademarks registered in the United States Patent and Trademark Office by Biblica, Inc.™

Scripture quotations taken from the (NASB®) New American Standard Bible®, Copyright © 1960, 1971, 1977, 1995 by The Lockman Foundation. Used by permission. All rights reserved. lockman.org

Scripture quotations marked MSG are taken from THE MESSAGE, copyright © 1993, 2002, 2018 by Eugene H. Peterson. Used by permission of NavPress. All rights reserved. Represented by Tyndale House Publishers, a Division of Tyndale House Ministries.

Printed in the United States of America

TABLE OF CONTENTS

From the Author 4

How to Use This Book 5

Introduction | In the Beginning 6

Kingdom of God Pattern 8
Lesson 1 | God Creates the World (Gen. 1:1-2:25) 9

Kingdom of God Perished 14
Lesson 2 | Man and Woman Sin (Gen. 3:1-24) 15
Lesson 3 | The Worldwide Flood (Gen 7:1-8:22 20

Kingdom of God Promised 24
Lesson 4 | God Makes Abram a Promise (Gen. 15:1-21) 25
Lesson 5 | Sarah Receives a Promise (Gen. 17:1-18:15, 21:1-7)) 29
Lesson 6 | Jacob Wrestles with God (Gen. 32:22-32) 32
Lesson 7 | God Prepares Joseph (Gen. 37:1-36) 36
Lesson 8 | God's Plan for Moses (Ex. 1:8-2:10) 40
Lesson 9 | Deliverance Through the Red Sea (Ex. 13:17-14:31) 43
Lesson 10 | God Reveals His Law at Mt. Sinai (Ex. 19:16-20:21) 47
Lesson 11 | Israel Follows God's Presence (Num. 9:1-23) 51
Lesson 12 | Israel Enters the Promised Land (Jsh. 5:13-6:27) 54

Kingdom of God Partial 58
Lesson 13 | God Raises Up Judges (Jdg. 2:6-23, 3:7-11) 59
Lesson 14 | Samson the Judge (Jdg. 16:4-31) 63
Lesson 15 | Samuel Hears God's Voice (I Sam. 3:1-4:11) 66
Lesson 16 | King David & Goliath (I Sam. 16:1-58) 69
Lesson 17 | King Solomon's Big Ask (I Kgs. 12:1-33) 72
Lesson 18 | Solomon Builds the Temple (I Kgs. 8:1-21, 54-62) 75

Kingdom of God Prophesied 78
Lesson 19 | Israel Divides (I Kgs. 12:1-33) 79
Lesson 20 | King Ahab & Elijah the Prophet (I Kgs. 16:29-17:24) 83
Lesson 21 | The Prophet Jonah (Jon. 1:1-2:10) 87
Lesson 22 | Israel Conquered by Assyria (II Kgs. 17:1-23) 91
Lesson 23 | King Joash & the Temple (II Chron. 24:1-27) 94
Lesson 24 | A Prophecy About David's Line (Is. 11:1-16) 97
Lesson 25 | Judah Conquered by Babylon (Jer. 52:1-30) 100
Lesson 26 | Ezekiel's Vision of Dry Bones (Ezek. 36:1-14) 103
Lesson 27 | Daniel in the Lion's Den (Dn. 6:1-28) 106
Lesson 28 | Return & Rebuild in Jerusalem (Ezra 3:1-13) 109
Bonus Lesson | Intertestamental Period (Gal. 4:4) 112
Lesson 29 | John the Baptist's Birth Foretold (Lk. 1:5-25) 115
Lesson 30 | Jesus' Birth Foretold (Lk 1:26-56) 118

Kingdom of God Present 121
Lesson 31 | Jesus is Born (Lk. 2:1-52) 122
Lesson 32 | The Baptism and Temptation of Jesus (Mt. 3:13-4:1) 126
Lesson 33 | The Sermon on the Mount (Mt. 5:1-26) 130
Lesson 34 | Jesus Feeds the Five Thousand (Jn. 6:1-15) 133
Lesson 35 | Jesus Heals a Blind Man (Jn. 9:1-41) 136
Lesson 36 | Jesus is the Way to God (Jn. 14:1-31) 139
Lesson 37 | The Death of Jesus (Mk. 15:1-47) 142
Lesson 38 | Jesus' Resurrection (Lk. 24:1-12) 145
Lesson 39 | The Holy Spirit is Promised (Acts 1:1-11) 148

Kingdom of God Proclaimed 151
Lesson 40 | The Holy Spirit Comes (Acts 2:1-41) 152
Lesson 41 | The Early Church (Acts 2:42-47) 156
Lesson 42 | Peter Heals a Crippled Man (Acts 3:1-11) 159
Lesson 43 | Saul Comes to Faith in Jesus (Acts 9:1-43) 162
Lesson 44 | Peter Visits Cornelius (Acts 10:1-48) 166
Lesson 45 | The Priority of Love (I Cor. 13:1-13) 169
Lesson 46 | The Servant Attitude of Jesus (Phil. 2:1-18) 172
Lesson 47 | The New Covenant (Heb. 8:1-13) 175
Lesson 48 | Examples of Strong Faith (Heb. 11:1-40) 178
Lesson 49 | The New Jerusalem (Rev. 21:1-22:6) 181

Kingdom of God Perfected 184
Lesson 50 | Jesus Will Return (Rev. 22:7-21) 185
Bonus Lesson | Bible Storyline Review 190

Where do I go from here? 192

Timeline Pages 193

FROM THE AUTHOR

Dear Reader,

I can't tell you how much it means to me that you are joining me in this journey to understand the Word of God. It's one I've been on for a long time. For thirty -some years I've served beside my husband Billy in ministry, supporting him in his work as Lead Pastor at Christ Community Church in West Chester, Pennsylvania.

Over the years, the Lord has impressed on me that my first ministry is to my husband, kids, and now grandkids. It is there that I enthusiastically invest most of my time. Secondarily, I have focused my time on teaching the Bible in various settings, applying my degree in education and years of studying the Bible to the work of teaching God's word. One of my favorite adventures has been the podcast my husband and I created together called "Everything Jesus." But my real heartbeat is small group Bible study. I absolutely love what happens when a few people join together around the Word of God, sharing their lives as God reveals His plan for them. It is a powerful thing!

As I've gathered around the Bible with hundreds of individuals over these decades, I have found that many struggle to understand the Bible as a whole. The book you hold in your hands contains the material I developed to meet this need. This Bible study has been used by hundreds over the last several years, and I've repeatedly heard that that they wished they'd had this tool sooner as it helped them to finally unlock the Bible. They are now able to see each part in vivid color, letting the Word transform them as they apply its truths. I am hopeful that it might serve you as well. Most importantly, I want you to see Jesus lifted up. And I want you to marvel as you watch God's kingdom plan unfold across history!

Blessings to you as you come to know the Savior more and more,
Kim Burch

"Yes, LORD,
Walking in the way of Your laws we wait for You.
Your name and renown are the desire of our hearts."
Isaiah 26:8 (NIV)

HOW TO USE THIS BOOK

Welcome to this Bible Study! Today, you are opening this book and in a few weeks you will close it understanding of the flow of the Bible - the unfolding of God's story across time. To get the most out of this time, look for the following key features in each lesson.

PRAYER MOMENT — Each lesson opens with a prayer prompt. This is a time to quiet yourself and invite God into your study of His Word. Think of it as inviting a good friend to sit down with you as you try to make sense out of life in this broken world. God has so much insight to offer you in His Word – ask Him to join you!

BIBLE PASSAGE — In each lesson you'll read the whole Bible passage first. Don't miss this step! It is vital to see each passage in its entirety before breaking it down and looking at the details. On this first pass, take note of the things that strike you by using the space provided. This is the beginning of what the Lord is revealing specifically to you through His Word.

If you're wondering what Bible translation to use, the New Living Translation has great readability and it was the version used in writing this book. Any Bible translation will be just fine, however when you are asked to fill in blanks on certain verses throughout this study it may be easiest to refer to the New Living Translation (which you can access on a Bible app or online if you don't own a print version). If you don't know how to look up verses in the Bible, there are many YouTube videos you can use to learn how.

QUESTIONS — It is here, in the bulk of the lesson, that you'll dive into the details of the Bible passage and move toward application of what you learn. Write your answers to the questions in the space provided. Don't rush through this because the facts you gather here will lead you to see how the passage relates to you today.

TIMELINE — As you move through this study, you'll be constructing a timeline chronicling the events of Biblical history. At the back of this book is the timeline template you'll fill in as you go. (Take a look at it now on page 193.) Don't worry, this study guide will direct you to what you'll need to write in each blank. At the end of each lesson there's a spot for you to check off once you've recorded that lesson's events.

PRAYER MOMENT — At the end of each lesson, you will again be prompted to pray. At this point, you are considering what you have learned and you're talking with the Lord about it as you close the lesson. Be sure to take the time to do this as it helps you solidify and process what you've learned.

Studying in a group? The group leader should access the Leader's Guide on our website at findingyourwaybiblestudy.com to get the most out of your discussions. It makes a difference to follow these methods for maximizing the impact of this book.

Studying by yourself? Try to find a friend who will study with you. If you don't get anyone to join you, look for nuggets of truth you can share with a friend or two along the way. Talking it through with others will help you remember what you learn. We have additional tips online, also on our website, findingyourwaybiblestudy.com.

INTRODUCTION

Open your Bible to Genesis 1:1. Write the first three words here:

"_____ _____ _____"

Think of a significant beginning in your life. How did it chart the course for your future? Did it bring difficulty or blessing? Was it a deliberate beginning, or just something incidental?

Well, for God, *this* beginning was the start of all that we now know in our physical world. In initiating this beginning, He was committing Himself to century upon century of involvement and engagement. It was a beginning He had thought about and planned for, not one launched into impulsively. We will see that when He started, He was putting Himself on the line, for He would one day sacrifice Himself for this creation He would make with His own hands. Amazing! Yet He began...

Genesis is a book about *many **beginnings***. The beginning of the world, of creation, is found in these pages. The beginning of work, marriage, sin, salvation, family, even language is here. What an adventure that we get to read a first-hand account of these things! The Bible, written by God through various people, gives us an account written by the One who was there all along - the One who is here now with you as you open His Word to study. Doesn't that make you eager to begin?!

Write a prayer to the Creator, dedicating this study to Him. (You can let Him know what you're excited about and what you're apprehensive about.)

Dear Lord...

Amen.

Having an overview of the Bible means you will understand the most significant events in the Bible, and what the Lord had been doing across history. This is going to give you a lifelong framework into which you can fit other events and Scriptures as you study in years ahead. I can't tell you how excited I am for you to build this framework for yourself.

Introduction

This is an adventure I have been on over the last several years. After studying the Bible in my own quiet times for thirty years in bits and pieces, I finally read it through from cover to cover. During that time, the Lord put into my hands an outstanding resource called *God's Big Picture** which helped me to look at segments of Scripture as specific phases of God's work, and this enabled me to finally retain the timeline. Now when I hear a sermon or read a specific Scripture I have an understanding of how it fits into the Bible, God's Story, as a whole. More importantly even, I discovered the amazing continuity of the Bible. It is one continuous story, about the One unchanging God.

Now, don't be intimidated if you are thinking, "I haven't studied the Bible for 30 years. How am I going to make sense of all of this?" My point is that wherever you are coming from, it is a good time for this study! This is really for anyone – whether you have been studying the Word for years, or are totally new to Bible study. We will take it a bit at a time, understand where each event fits in to God's timeline, and when you close this book at the end of 50 lessons you will have your very own overview.

What experiences have you had in studying the Bible?

What have you enjoyed about it?

What have you found difficult?

PRAYER MOMENT

Wherever you are coming from, whatever your experience has been, God desires to meet you in His Word. Psalm 119:18 says, "Open my eyes to see wonderful things in your law." The "law" was the first five books of the Bible – the only part available to them at the time. You have all 66 books of the Bible sitting beside you right now, and God intends to show you wonderful things through all of those books! Pray right now, asking the Lord to do this work in your life.

If you are new to prayer, you might pray something like this:

Dear Lord,
I pray that you would open my eyes to see wonderful things in the Bible. Thank you for providing such an amazing Book for me to learn from. Help me to learn about You as I read; and help me to learn about myself. I commit the upcoming weeks of Bible study to you.
In Jesus' name, Amen

* I will be using the basic concepts provided by Vaughan Roberts' in his book *God's Big Picture, Tracing the Storyline of the Bible* (InterVarsity Press, 2002) for the theme we will trace in this Bible study.

KINGDOM OF GOD
PATTERN

LESSON ONE

Now, let's begin...Open your Bible to Genesis 1.

PRAYER MOMENT

We always want to invite the Lord to participate with us as we read His Word. Take a moment to pray before you read right now.

Open my eyes, Lord, to see wonderful things in Your Word.

BIBLE PASSAGE

Read Genesis 1:1-2:25 and use the space below to record any questions it brings to mind or things you notice.

As we work through this study you are going to construct your own timeline. Using the pages in the back of this book, you will be given numbered spaces to note events as they unfold. So here we are at the very first one.

Looking at Genesis 1:1, who existed before creation? _____

Yes, God was in existence in eternity past, before anything that we now know or can see. Amazing, isn't it?

On line #1 on your **TIMELINE** (located in the back of this book) write **"GOD"**.

Go back over Genesis 1:3 – 2:4 and fill in the chart on the following page.

Lesson One

	What God Made	How He Made It	How did He feel about what He had made?	Are any instructions given about this part of creation?
Day 1 (Vs. 3-5)				
Day 2 (Vs. 6-8)				
Day 3 (Vs. 9-13)				
Day 4 (Vs. 14-19)				
Day 5 (Vs. 20-23)				
Day 6 (Vs. 24-31)				
Day 7 (Vs. 2:1-4)				

In Genesis 2:7 the writer goes back and gives us more detail about Day 6 of creation. Add that information into your chart.

Two significant events happen in Adam's life in Genesis 2.

EVENT ONE: v. 15 – What assignment was Adam given?

vv. 19-20 – What does he do as part of this assignment?

That's curious, isn't it? Creation was perfectly formed, but Adam was assigned work to do within it. What does that tell us about God's plan for mankind?

EVENT TWO: So Adam undertook his work, and named all of the creatures. And as he saw them walk by, each with a mate, Adam realized he was alone. Isn't God good? He was methodically revealing to Adam his need: a mate!

So often God works in this way, revealing to us a need we have, showing us we cannot meet it on our own. Then *He* comes with the solution – the answer to our need. And we know it is a provision directly from His hand. Read verses 18-25 and see how this unfolded in Adam's life.
God was doing a great work here – the beginning of family!

How did God describe this new creation called "woman?" (vs. 18)

How did Adam describe her? (vs. 23)

Lesson One

So there it is - God's creation. Beautiful, isn't it? Pristine, perfect, unblemished. Imagine it! Picture the most beautiful place you have ever been. Envision the details of God's creation there.

And on top of the all the beauty there in the Garden of Eden, God's presence was right there with them. This was how He intended it to be! You see, God's plan was for us to enjoy life *with* Him. He has such a Father's heart that He wanted to have children to share His goodness with. He has wonderful and perfect plans, like a good King, and He wanted a people with whom He would carry out those wonderful plans. His people would follow His leadership and enjoy the blessing of His presence and His protection.

Use the chart on the previous page to guide you as you continue to fill in your timeline. We'll do similar check-ins throughout the course of this study.

PRAYER MOMENT

What can you learn from looking back at this, the very beginning of God's Story? What does it tell you about how you should live your life? Jot your thoughts here, and then pray about these things.

☐ *Check here when you have filled out your timeline with the new entries from this lesson.*

BIBLICAL THEME:
THE KINGDOM OF GOD

Over the next weeks, as we study the Bible together, we will watch God's kingdom plan unfold. What has He been doing across time? What is the point of His engagement with mankind? What is His intended plan? These are questions we will be finding the answer to.

As we study, it is helpful to trace a unifying theme throughout the Bible. So, let's begin here in Genesis 1 and 2. This is the opening Chapter in God's story. Here we see:

God's **PEOPLE**
in God's **PLACE**
under God's **RULE**
enjoying God's **BLESSING**

We will keep looking at these four markers as we watch God's kingdom work throughout scripture, so we will call our theme the **KINGDOM OF GOD.** Specifically, the Kingdom of God is "the sphere in which God's rule is gladly accepted," says Pastor Alistar Begg. As we study, you will find that God perseveres with man across time until His beautiful plan unfolds perfectly.

At certain points in our study we will pause to look at what is going on with God's kingdom work. Let's assess what's going on at this point in the story, here in Genesis 1 and 2, by pondering these questions:

God's **PEOPLE:** Who are God's People here?

God's **PLACE:** Are the people in the place where God intended them to be?

God's **RULE:** How are they doing at following the lead of the King? Are they obeying Him?

God's **BLESSING:** Are the people enjoying God's blessing? How do we see that?

We can remember what God is doing with His people during this phase of Biblical history by watching these indicators: God's people, God's place, God's rule, God's blessing. This phase of history is the PATTERN of the Kingdom of God. This is life as He intended it to be!

☐ *Check here when you have written "Kingdom of God Pattern" in Oval A on your Timeline.*

KINGDOM OF GOD
PERISHED

LESSON TWO

Genesis is a book all about beginnings. What beginnings have we seen so far? List them here:

We will see another beginning today…a tragic one: the beginning of sin. Our human hearts cry out constantly about the brokenness in our world. "Why do bad things happen?" "Why is there so much pain?" "Why is every worthwhile thing I set out to do so difficult?" What additional hard questions do you ask?

"Where is God?" we ask. The answer is that God is where He has always been – on His throne; He *is* King. He created a world that reflected His character: beautiful and perfect. But the choices of Adam and Eve marred that perfection and introduced all of the pain and brokenness we now experience. Let's see how that all happened.

PRAYER MOMENT

Ask the Lord to give you new insight into how temptation comes into your life as you read today.

BIBLE PASSAGE

Read Genesis 3:1-24 and use the space below to record any questions it brings to mind or things you notice.

The serpent here was actually Satan in some sort of visible form. Later in Scripture we read that our enemy roams around looking for people to devour. He comes to steal, kill and destroy. He has been at that same plan from the beginning. God creates, Satan seeks to destroy. God brings life, Satan tries to kill. God gives, Satan steals. But we should never think God and Satan are equal and opposite forces. God is sovereign over this enemy and will one day defeat him.

Lesson Two

Look how Satan came on the scene: (Gen. 3:1)

Who did he come to?

What did he say?

Now compare that to:

Who was originally given the instruction from God?
(Gen. 2:15-17)

What was the original instruction about the Tree of the Knowledge of Good and Evil?

Interesting. Satan came to the woman, who had only second-hand knowledge of God's command. She could have gone to Adam to check out what was being said, or better yet, she could have called on God to make sure she understood accurately. But she tried to handle it on her own.

What does this tell you about what *you* should do in order to face temptation without succumbing?

Notice that Satan didn't even accurately quote God's command to Eve. Unfortunately, Eve did not do any better – she responded by also misquoting the instruction. **Satan always attacks at the Word of God.** Rewrite that last sentence below and think about it for a minute.

The way Satan can succeed in drawing us to sin is by leading us to believe that God and His Word are not to be trusted - that God is flat-out wrong about what is best for us. Look at the story as it continues in Genesis 3:4-5.

"The Lord is depriving you of all the good stuff," Satan conveys. "Do this and you will be like God." Look back on Genesis 1:27. How had God originally created Adam and Eve?

The enemy was trying to make them believe they didn't have God's image on them, and that they needed to get something God was too stingy to give. How did Eve make her decision in vs. 6?

> She saw ... she wanted ... she took ... she gave. She would not allow herself to remain dependent on God; she would take matters into her own hands. And then she would put the fruit into Adam's hand. This is the enemy's strategy – to convince one, who would then influence and convince others.

What did Adam and Eve feel in vs. 7? (Compare that to Gen. 2:25)

What did they do because of this feeling?

> They felt the need to cover-up because of the shame they felt. But this cover-up wasn't sufficient to keep God from seeing them for who they were. ***God*** would be the only One who could cover their sin.

How did God cover them in verse 21?

> God provided a sacrifice to cover their sin. Blood had to be shed. This was a foreshadowing of what Jesus would ultimately do for us when He came.

Because of their sin…
What consequences fell to Eve, and to women? (vs. 16)

GOD
WORLD
MAN
WOMAN

Kingdom of God
PATTERN

5. FALL

Kingdom of God
PERISHED

Lesson Two

What consequences fell to Adam, and to men? (vs. 17 – 19)

So the focus of the curse is targeted at two vital parts of life: family and work. And then sin's repercussions ripple out and touch so much of what we experience. Adam and Eve would see this play out before their eyes in the years ahead.

PRAYER MOMENT

We need to be wise about the ways Satan comes to us with temptation. Look back over this lesson and mark the ways the enemy came with temptation to Adam and Eve. As you review these, pray through each, asking God to help you resist the devil when he strives to steal, kill and destroy in your life.

☐ *Check here when you have filled out your timeline with the new entry from this lesson.*

BIBLICAL THEME:
THE KINGDOM OF GOD

Again, let's look at the Kingdom of God theme at this point in the story.

God's **PEOPLE**
in God's **PLACE**
under God's **RULE**
enjoying God's **BLESSING**

God's **PEOPLE:** Who are God's People here?

God's **PLACE:** Are the people in the place where God intended them to be?

God's **RULE:** How are they doing at following the lead of the King? Are they obeying Him?

God's **BLESSING:** Are the people enjoying God's blessing? How do we see that?

This is most certainly not the beautiful picture we saw in chapters 1 and 2 of Genesis. The **PATTERN** of the kingdom in those chapters **PERISHED** when Adam and Eve chose independence from God.

☐ *Check here when you have written "Kingdom of God Perished" in Oval B on your Timeline.*

LESSON THREE

In our last lesson we saw the beginning of sin and brokenness in the world. Sin separates. Sin spoils. Sin spreads. Today as we open our Bibles we have actually jumped about 1,500 years ahead from the time of Adam and Eve to the time of Noah. The Bible is a unique book in that it slows down and examines a brief moment in history, and then speeds up and spans centuries in just a few pages. Creatively, God chooses which parts of the story to provide for us, always making sure we get every detail we need to understand the big picture of who He is and what He is doing: redeeming a people for Himself. He is building a kingdom of His very own.

PRAYER MOMENT

"Lord, let me see in this story how sin separates, sin spoils, and sin spreads. However, help me to remember that You are always at work. You always keep a remnant of people who will follow You."

BIBLE PASSAGE

Read Genesis 6:5 – 8:22 and use the space below to record any questions it brings to mind or things you notice.

Let's begin by focusing on the details provided in chapter 6. Here at the beginning of the story, what do we know about Noah? What are we told, and what can we infer based on his life? (vs. 6:8-9, 22)

What was the culture around Noah like? (vs. 6:5-7, 11-13)

20 Finding Your Way

Fill in the blanks using the verses referenced:

While being surrounded by a culture in which "_____ they thought or imagined was consistently and totally evil,"
(vs. 5 NLT)

"Noah did _____ _____ as God had commanded him."
(vs. 22 NLT)

Noah had spent his life training for an assignment like this, a time when God would come to him with a project that required accurate obedience. How do you think Noah did this?

What specific things can you do to be ready for God to use you?

What can we learn about God from Genesis 7:1? What does this verse show us about Him?

If you are familiar with this story you may know that it rained for forty days and forty nights. That makes us think that Noah was on the boat a little over a month. Not such a big deal, really. But as you read it now, notice how long this actually went on.

Genesis 7:11 - By looking at the days listed we can piece together that they entered the boat on the ____th day of the _____ month in one year and didn't leave until the 27th day of the second month the following year (Gen. 8:13-14). They were on the boat for over a year! A long obedience in the same direction was required to make it through.

What areas in your life right now are requiring a long obedience in the same direction?

Lesson Three

For Noah and his family, their long obedience had gone on for many years. Countless sacrifices had been made to carry out all that God had asked of them. But, as is always the case, this **obedience brought blessing!**

The second part of verse 23 tells us – "The _____ people who _____ were Noah and those with him _____ _____ _____."

Were there various options for survival? ____ yes ____ no

How could a person escape death?

Again, here in this first book of the Bible, we see a foreshadowing of God's salvation plan. One's survival was dependent on reaching out and accepting the <u>only</u> "life raft." There were not options. Believing God meant that Noah obeyed and went into God's only deliverance tool. The same is true in salvation today. We must reach out and accept the <u>only</u> One through whom we can receive deliverance: Jesus Christ.

Chapter 8 ends with Noah offering a sacrifice to God in verses 20 – 22. Why do you think he did this?

What other time in our study so far have we seen animal sacrifice? What was its purpose then? (Hint: look back to Lesson Two where we studied Genesis 3:21)

In verses 21-22 what does the Lord promise?

What three words might you use to sum up Noah's life as seen in these chapters?

PRAYER MOMENT

Again, let's reflect on Genesis 6:22, "Noah did **everything exactly** as God had commanded him." The Lord used Noah for an enormous project that literally saved mankind, and it began with Noah obeying _accurately_. God can work with and through someone who obeys Him precisely and thoroughly. Where in your life do you need to obey _accurately_ what the Lord has asked? Pray about that now.

☐ *Check here when you have filled out your timeline with the new entries from this lesson.*

KINGDOM OF GOD
PROMISED

LESSON FOUR

> ## PRAYER MOMENT
>
> *"You have done what you promised, for you are always true to your word." Nehemiah 9:8b.* Pray that you will learn more about our trustworthy, faithful, righteous God today as you study.

As Genesis unfolds, in chapter 11 the people unite to build a great tower. On the surface, it looks like a harmless endeavor. But God had instructed them to fill the earth, spreading out to **make His name great** and instead, they unite in an effort to all stay in one place and **make their own names great**. God interrupts their plan, destroying their solidarity by creating a diversity of languages. Since they can't understand one another, they relinquish their tower aspirations, divide up into groups according to language, and disperse into various regions. Out of the people groups which develop, God chooses one through which to demonstrate His goodness to the world: the line of Abram. At this point in Genesis, we zoom in and follow this family for four generations.

Let's look at where this begins with Abram in Genesis 12:1-9.

WHAT GOD SAYS:

Vs. 1: What does God instruct Abram to do?

Vs. 2, 7: What does God promise the results will be?

HOW ABRAM RESPONDS:

Vs. 4-6: What does Abram do in response to God's instructions?

Vs. 7-8: How does Abram respond to the Lord?

Glance back over the left column above. Notice how demanding the instructions that God made were…and how weighty the promises were.

Now look again at the right column. How did Abram respond? He looks like someone who the Lord can use, doesn't he? What do you see here that tells you that?

Lesson Four

BIBLE PASSAGE

Read Genesis 15:1-21 and use the space below to record any questions it brings to mind or things you notice.

Look at these verses as you did with Genesis 12, putting God's words and Abram's responses side-by-side.

WHAT GOD SAYS:

Vs. 1: What does God promise?

Vs. 4: What does God promise?

How many descendants would Abram have?

Vs. 7: What else does God promise?

HOW ABRAM RESPONDS:

Vs. 2: What problem does Abram see?

Vs. 6: How does Abram react to this unbelievable promise?

Vs. 8: How does Abram react to this unbelievable promise?

Sounds like a bit of a contradiction, doesn't it? "Sovereign Lord" (which is like saying "All-Powerful Master") "how can I be sure this is actually going to happen?" You can be sure, Abram, because the Lord is the One who is in control, and He is all-powerful, omnipotent…sovereign.

The Lord committed Himself to this promise through a covenant ceremony which unfolded before Abram's eyes in verses 9-26. This promise is an *unconditional* promise, not contingent on Abram, but dependent upon God alone. God would fulfill the covenant He committed Himself to here, and nothing could prevent it.

What details in these verses do you think indicate that this covenant was dependent upon God alone?

PRAYER MOMENT

What is a seemingly impossible situation that you are facing right now?

Ponder your seemingly impossible situation in light of Psalm 138:8:

"The LORD (it's His job)
will work out (it takes work)
His plan (…always the best!)
for my life (He has taken notice of even me!)
for your faithful love, O Lord, endures forever. (It is all grounded in His persevering love)
Do not abandon me for you made me." (He won't – He's more interested in seeing this fulfilled than I am even!)

Now spend a moment praying about the truths in this Psalm.

☐ *Check here when you have filled out your timeline with the new entries from this lesson.*

GOD

WORLD
MAN
WOMAN

Kingdom of God
PATTERN

FALL
FLOOD
7. TOWER OF BABEL

Kingdom of God
PERISHED

8. ABRAM

Kingdom of God
PROMISED

Lesson Four

BIBLICAL THEME:
THE KINGDOM OF GOD

Remember the theme that we are tracing throughout this study is the Kingdom of God. We are looking at:

God's _____

in God's _____

under God's _____

enjoying God's _____

So let's evaluate what's going on with the Kingdom of God at this point in the story:

God's **PEOPLE:** Who are God's People here?

God's **PLACE:** Are the people in the place where God intended them to be?

God's **RULE:** How are they doing at following the lead of the King? Are they obeying Him?

God's **BLESSING:** Are the people enjoying God's blessing? How do we see that?

The Bible opened with a beautiful view of the **Kingdom of God Pattern**, but just a few pages into the story we saw that the **Kingdom of God Perished**. God does not give up on the plan, however. He reaches down and chooses Abram as the man through whom He will begin to restore His kingdom. It will take many years for all that the Lord is speaking of to come to fruition. At this point in the story, we just have the **Kingdom of God Promised**. The promises to Abram indicate that God will again have a people, who are in His chosen place, who live under His rule, and enjoy His blessing.

As we read the wide-sweeping promises God makes to Abram, they sound unachievable. But seemingly impossible things are no barrier for the Lord. He will accomplish what He plans, regardless of how it appears to us.

☐ *Check here when you have written "Kingdom of God Promised" in Oval C on your Timeline.*

LESSON FIVE

PRAYER MOMENT

Pray that you will more clearly understand the truth in this verse as you study today: "My grace is all you need. My power works best in weakness. So now I am glad to boast about my weaknesses, so that the power of Christ can work through me." (II Corinthians 12:9)

BIBLE PASSAGE

Read Genesis 17:1-18:15 and use the space below to record any questions it brings to mind or things you notice.

Have you ever gotten tired of waiting for something and taken matters into your own hands? Well, that's where Abram and Sarai found themselves as they awaited the promise of a son to become a reality. After years of waiting, they caved in. Rather than continuing to wait on God, they followed an accepted cultural practice using Sarai's handmaiden as a stand-in for her, a sort of surrogate mother. And a son, named Ishmael, was born to them.

The line of reasoning Sarai employed here goes like this:

You see, the *wait* exceeded their *faith*. But what God was calling them to went like this:

Abram and Sarai had gone outside of God's instructions and had taken this shortcut. Now, in chapter 17, Abram was 99 as the Lord came again to him and reiterated the covenant promise. God described Himself to Abram, saying He is "El Shaddai." Can you imagine it? Hearing God Himself explain who He is? And this description is filled with weighty implications. It means "God Almighty" and points to the fact that God provides, nourishes, and sustains. God cares for His people, blessing them abundantly.

Abundance…blessing…provision…power. This was something Abram would have to experience personally if he was ever to see this promise fulfilled in the way God intended. What was highly unlikely for Abram at age 75 now felt entirely impossible. Time had only cemented the conclusion that this simply couldn't happen.

Lesson Five

So, these chapters provide for us a glimpse into what unbelief looks like. Let's look at the responses of Abraham and Sarah as our merciful God proclaimed His promise to them again.

Genesis 17:

Vs. 17-18: What did Abraham do? What was he focusing on?

Vs. 19, 21: What specifics of the promise did God clarify? (Who? When?)

Genesis 18:

Vs. 10: What specifics of the promise did God clarify? (Who? When?)

Vs. 11-15: What did Sarah do? What was she focusing on?

Abraham and Sarah needed to grapple with the fact that it wasn't what was visible that mattered, but what was unseen – God's almighty power and covenant commitment. Remember: this was a covenant completely dependent on God. Unconditional. Likewise, in *your* life, you need to:

→ Not look at practical limitations!
→ Not offer substitute shortcuts to God when His way looks impossible!

If you're the one chosen for the task you need to bow and not laugh. The point isn't for God to use a logical and perfect tool for the job. The point is for His almighty power to be demonstrated through you: a weak and insufficient tool.

Where in your life do you tend to look at your practical limitations? In what areas do you believe your limitations are too great for God to be able to work?

Is there any area in which you have offered a substitute shortcut to God?

Now read Genesis 21:1-7. Rewrite verse 1 here:

"The Lord _____

and did for Sarah _____."

What specifics of the promise had God fulfilled here? (Who? When?)

And Sarah declared, "God has brought me _____.

All who hear about this will _____ with me." (Vs. 6)

There was a lot of laughter going on in the lives of these two characters. They laughed in unbelief at first, but now they laughed in delight. There is joy (and humor!) in being used by God in impossible ways. Abraham and Sarah would name this child "Isaac" – don't miss it, his name means "laughter."

PRAYER MOMENT

Romans 4:20-21 says, *"Abraham never wavered in believing God's promise. In fact, his faith grew stronger, and in this he brought glory to God. He was fully convinced that God is able to do whatever He promises."*

Through his experiences Abraham grew strong in faith and became fully persuaded that what God had promised He was able also to perform.

Take some time in prayer to remember areas in your life which once seemed ominous and impossible, yet you have seen God come through powerfully (ex. illness, relationships, projects, losses). List them here:

☐ *Check here when you have filled out your timeline with the new entries from this lesson.*

GOD
WORLD
MAN
WOMAN

Kingdom of God **PATTERN**

FALL
FLOOD
TOWER OF BABEL

Kingdom of God **PERISHED**

ABRAM
(ABRAHAM)
9. ISHMAEL
10. ISAAC

Kingdom of God **PROMISED**

LESSON SIX

> ## PRAYER MOMENT
>
> In Exodus 33:12-13 Moses said to the Lord, *"You have said You know me by name and I have found favor in Your eyes. Teach me Your ways so I may continue to find favor in Your eyes."*
>
> Thank the Lord now that He knows you *by name* and pray that He will teach you today.

Do you know the meaning of your first name? Or your last name? Do you have any nickname that you have been given? Why were you given that nickname?

Think back on a few of the names we have encountered in the Biblical story so far. Do you recall any of the meanings associated with these names?

Abram: Sarah:

Abraham: Isaac:

Sarai: El Shaddai:

At birth, when parents place a name on a child, they may be portraying who they hope the baby will become. In a similar way, nicknames are applied to a person based on some trait noticed in the individual. However, when God gives a name, it is so much more significant. His assignment of a name flows from His omniscience, His knowledge of everything. He *knows* who this person will become, who He is designing them to be. It is not just wishful thinking; it is a sure reality. When God discloses part of His own character to us through one of *His* names, it reveals a facet of His personality that we can consistently count on. It is not something that will come and go. All of His character is perpetually active as He works.

Today's Scripture reading is heavy with meaning, as we see God assign a new name to another Old Testament individual. What we will watch unfold as we read had implications when it occurred and continues to today – thousands of years later.

Abraham…Isaac…Jacob

Maybe you have heard these three names listed together before. Quite frequently in the Bible God identifies Himself as "the God of Abraham, Isaac and Jacob." (Abraham gave birth to Isaac who gave birth to Jacob.) Remember God was working out his promise, His covenant, by drawing out a family line through whom He would accomplish His salvation plan. We are calling this the "**Kingdom of God Promised**." Where is this all going? Well, this family line will eventually bring Jesus into the world!

Lesson Six

For now, let's zero in on Jacob, Isaac's son, as he is the next significant character in our story.

BIBLE PASSAGE

Read Genesis 32:22-32 and use the space below to record any questions it brings to mind or things you notice.

Jacob is not a stellar individual at this point in the story. In fact, his name actually means "Deceiver." Yet, as we saw with Abraham and Sarah, God will use whomever He chooses to use, whether or not they come to the assignment with the raw goods which would seem to be necessary.

Let's examine a few scenes from Jacob's life so we can get a picture of who he is.

GRASPER...

When Jacob was born (Genesis 25:24-26), how did he come on the scene?

This baby was named "Jacob" which sounds like the Hebrew words for "heel" and "deceiver." This was the one trait his parents saw at his birth, and they noted it in his name. (The name of the other twin wasn't much better: Esau means "hairy." Apparently, these parents didn't have much creativity.)

GRASPER... *SCHEMER...*

When Jacob's father was on his deathbed (Genesis 27:5-17), what did Jacob scheme for?

GRASPER... SCHEMER... *DECEIVER...*

As the scene continued (Genesis 27:11-29), what are all the deceptive things Jacob did?

When Esau found out, "Esau exclaimed, 'No wonder his name is Jacob, for now he has cheated me twice. First he took my rights as the firstborn, and now he has stolen my blessing'..." Genesis 27:36.

Kingdom of God Promised 33

Lesson Six

GRASPER... SCHEMER... DECEIVER... *DECEIVED...*

To avoid any retaliation from his brother, Jacob promptly fled to Paddan-Aram, his mother's hometown. He had the "luck" of finding his Uncle Laban there and fell in love with one of his daughters. But the tables were about to turn on Jacob.

In what ways did the tables turn on Jacob in Genesis 29:18-25?

GRASPER... SCHEMER... DECEIVER... DECEIVED... *RENAMED...*

> *"Even in the womb, Jacob struggled with his brother; when he became a man, he even fought with God."*
> Hosea 12:3

With Jacob's backstory in mind, we now come to today's reading in Genesis 32. Grab ahold of the setting here. After stealing Esau's birthright, Jacob lived in fear of his brother Esau's vengeance. But now Jacob was on his way back to Shechem where his brother still lived. Although he had been away for many years, he was consumed with fear about what he was going to encounter. On this night, Jacob sent his whole family and all his worldly goods across the river and slept alone in a deserted place. Alone, without all he had schemed to have, suddenly he was awakened...

Summarize what happened in this scene in Genesis 32:22-32 before Jacob was renamed.

So let's review what we've seen. Jacob was a **grasper**, **schemer**, and **deceiver**, who was eventually **deceived**. Mercifully, God did not leave him defined by his sin and brokenness. Instead, God **renamed** Jacob.

Let's soak in the meaning of this new name which Jacob was given. "Israel" can mean "wrestles with God" and can also mean "God fights." Surely we have seen both of these in the scene we are studying today: Jacob wrestled and God fought. But these connotations go beyond the scene at hand and foreshadow the history which would unfold for God's people, the Israelites.

WRESTLES WITH GOD...

From what you know about the history of Israel in the rest of the Bible, in what ways have the Israelites "wrestled with God?"

How about in contemporary history, how has the nation of Israel "wrestled with God?"

34 Finding Your Way

GOD FIGHTS...

But we don't want to miss the many ways "God fights" for the Israelite people, both in the Bible and contemporary history. Note those here:

PRAYER MOMENT

How about you? Are there areas in your life right now where you are **wrestling with God**? Are you grasping, scheming, maybe even deceiving, rather than submitting to God's plan and provision? List them here, then lay them before God in prayer.

In what ways throughout your life have you seen **God fight** on your behalf? Write them here, and as you write, praise God for His willingness to fight for you.

Later, in Genesis 35:10-12, God appears again to Jacob and reminds him:

> "<u>Your name is</u> Jacob, but you will not be called Jacob any longer.
> From now on your name will be Israel." So God renamed him Israel.
>
> "<u>I am</u> El Shaddai – 'God Almighty.'
> Be fruitful and multiply. You will become a great nation, even many nations.
> Kings will be among your descendants!
> And I will give you the land I once gave to Abraham and Isaac.
> Yes, I will give it to you and your descendants after you."

☐ *Check here when you have filled out your timeline with the new entries from this lesson.*

Timeline:
- GOD
- WORLD
- MAN
- WOMAN — *Kingdom of God* **PATTERN**
- FALL
- FLOOD
- TOWER OF BABEL — *Kingdom of God* **PERISHED**
- ABRAM *(ABRAHAM)*
- ISHMAEL
- ISAAC
- **11. JACOB (ISRAEL)** — *Kingdom of God* **PROMISED**

LESSON SEVEN

PRAYER MOMENT

Think about the winding path the Lord has had you on throughout your life. Pray that He will use the twists and turns you are experiencing right now.

BIBLE PASSAGE

Read Genesis 37:1-36 and use the space below to record any questions it brings to mind or things you notice.

As this chapter opens, the focus turns to Joseph, son of Jacob, who was now 17. Over the years that have passed, family tension had been brewing so it was now almost palpable. There were 12 sons in this family, born to four different mothers, with Jacob fathering them all.

What do we see Joseph doing in verse 2?

How did his father feel about him, and what did he do? (Vs. 3)

And the result was… (Vs. 4):

It goes something like this:

12 Sons + 4 Moms + 1 Dad + Tattling + Favoritism = FAMILY TENSION

Clearly, this was a disaster waiting to happen! Yet somehow Joseph was oblivious to it. He had some amazing dreams and was eager to share them with his brothers. Surely they would be delighted for him, these brothers who couldn't say a kind word to him. Perhaps he hoped it would gain him some respect.

What was similar between his two dreams? (Vs. 5-9)

Lesson Seven

Notice how Joseph's family reacted to his dreams:

Response of his brothers (Vs. 8, 11):   Response of his father (Vs. 10-11):

And so, the family rift grew greater. Yet Jacob was oblivious to what was festering beneath the surface. "Go and see how your brothers and the flocks are getting along, then come back and bring me a report," his father says. (Translation: "Go spy on your brothers and come tattle to me about them.") Not a good scheme for a father to pull his son into.

Throughout Joseph's life he experienced many varying roles or jobs. What "job" did he have at this point? (What was the role he served his father in?) Write your answer below:

JOB #1: _____ (_____)

In the parenthesis next to the line write a word that describes what you see in Joseph's character here.

In verses 18-28, how did the brothers react to the sight of Joseph when they saw him in the distance? What plans were suggested?

The brothers agreed that it would be a good idea to gain as much as possible from the situation. "Sweet revenge," they thought. Yes, they'd get rid of him and get some cash at the same time. Listen to them. They call him 'the dreamer,' 'the boy.' Joseph had lost his personhood to them; he was nothing more than those ridiculous dreams and that obnoxious robe.
Do you relate? Can you think of someone who has annoyed you so much, or has made your life so difficult that you began to think of them as less-than? Maybe secretly it would delight you if they suffered a little...or a lot?

It's sobering to see how that kind of thinking can fester into revenge.

In verses 27-28 Joseph had been utterly demoted in status. So, what was his "job" now? (Write this on the line below.) And what character flaws might this have been working out of Joseph's character? (Put inside parenthesis.)

JOB #2: _____ (_____)

What a painful path Joseph has traveled thus far. Why do you think God used such a difficult journey for Joseph?

Joseph had been favored by his father and had played into that role himself by telling on his brothers whenever there was opportunity, and his father was happy to use him for this. However, God had a much more significant job for him. For the Lord to get this teenager's proud, spoiled, favored attitude straight he would need to be humbled, neglected and forgotten. This would prepare him to be used for God's assignment - a process that would take 14 years.

Lesson Seven

Continue in this unfolding drama and read Genesis 39. Again, take note of the jobs Joseph held as outlined in these verses:

(Genesis 39:1-6) JOB #3: _____ (_____)

(Genesis 39:22) JOB #4: _____ (_____)

What character traits are being developed or demonstrated through these jobs? Write these in the parenthesis above.

*"The LORD was with Joseph,
so he succeeded in everything he did as he served in the home of his Egyptian master." (Genesis 39:2)*

*"But the LORD was with Joseph in the prison
and showed him his faithful love.
And the LORD made Joseph a favorite with the prison warden." (Genesis 39:21)*

*"The LORD was with him
and caused everything he did to succeed." (Genesis 39:23)*

These verses feel like rays of hope in what must have seemed like a dark time. **Underline what is similar between these three verses.**

In your life right now, can you think of any rays of hope: places of God's presence, or areas where you are perhaps experiencing success, in spite of darkness which persists in another area?

Read Genesis 40 and note what role Joseph plays here, along with the character trait being cultivated.

JOB #5: _____ (_____)

*Then "...they forgot all about Joseph, never giving him another thought...
Two full years later...(the Cup Bearer said) "today I have been reminded...
there was a young Hebrew man, we told him our dreams, and he told us what each of our dreams meant."
(Genesis 40:23, 41:1, 9, 12)*

In a flash, Joseph was whisked out of the dungeon to advise Pharaoh about Pharaoh's own troubling dream. As had been the case at each turn in Joseph's life, the Lord's abiding presence was vividly evident. "Can we find anyone else like this man so obviously filled with the Spirit of God?" (Gen. 41:38). Impressed by this young Hebrew slave "Pharaoh said to Joseph, "I hereby put you in charge of the entire land of Egypt...No one will lift a hand or foot in the entire land of Egypt without your approval." With those words, Joseph was commissioned with the task of preparing the country for the impending famine.

JOB #6: _____ (_____)

Years passed and Joseph married, had children, and succeeded brilliantly in his work. He had put his brothers behind him. Well, eventually the famine became so oppressive in the land of Canaan that those brothers came to Egypt to beg for food. There they unknowingly came face-to-face with the brother they abused and discarded 22 years before.

Joseph wrestled through feelings of hurt, anger and resentment, but was eventually ready to extend to his brothers the mercy and grace God had planned. Read Genesis 45:3-8 and note here what you think are key phrases in Joseph's words to his brothers.

What would you say Joseph's "job" was here? And what character trait do you see him demonstrate?

JOB #7: _____ (_____)

So, Joseph's 11 brothers, his father and all the extended family came to live in Egypt under the protective care of Joseph. This would, indeed, save their lives at that time. But it would eventually come to mean something entirely different for the Israelite people.

PRAYER MOMENT

Glance back through today's lesson at all the character the Lord worked into (and out of) Joseph's life as he walked this winding path. What are some traits you know the Lord is trying to prune out of your character?

Realize that the Lord is working on this in preparation for what He knows is coming in your life. Write a prayer about this below, and yield to His agenda as you pray.

☐ *Check here when you have filled out your timeline with the new entry from this lesson.*

GOD
WORLD — Kingdom of God **PATTERN**
MAN
WOMAN

FALL
FLOOD — Kingdom of God **PERISHED**
TOWER OF BABEL

ABRAM *(ABRAHAM)*
ISHMAEL — Kingdom of God **PROMISED**
ISAAC
JACOB *(ISRAEL)*
12. JOSEPH

LESSON EIGHT

> ## PRAYER MOMENT
>
> Take a few minutes to praise the Lord in prayer for the good things He is doing through your life right now.
>
> ## BIBLE PASSAGE
>
> Read Exodus 1:1-2:10 and use the space below to record any questions it brings to mind or things you notice.

What motivated this new king to enslave the Israelite people? (Vs. 8-10)

Reflecting on our theme of the Kingdom of God, consider what is going on at this point. God's people are not in His place at all, instead they find themselves in Egypt – not God's chosen place. And rather than experiencing God's blessing, they are experiencing slavery. On the surface, it looks like the plan is failing. Yet, God is at work, preserving His people even in this place.

Our reading today includes two of the most forgotten Biblical characters: Shiphrah and Puah. What was their motivation in what they did? (Exodus 1:17)

Don't you just love those two spunky ladies? All throughout Scripture we find that the Lord has always had a remnant of His people who are faithful to obey Him. The Israelite nation could have easily been absorbed into the prevailing culture of Egypt and lost their distinction as God's people. These women could have caved into the pressure of these oppressive rulers and killed off Abraham's family line. But we see these two courageously, faithfully obeying, and the results are significant.

This is the first of a number of times in history when Satan sought to eradicate the Jewish people. Remember, the enemy always is at work to steal, kill, and destroy, in hopes of opposing God's plan of grace. We see in these opening chapters of Exodus how the Lord works to move His plan forward by using a few faithful people.

Courage was also needed by another Israelite woman we meet in Exodus 2.

Who was she? And what did she do? (Exodus 2:1-3)

In your life, what is an area of obedience that requires courage right now?

> "Years passed, and the king of Egypt died. But the Israelites continued to groan under their burden of slavery. They cried out for help, and their cry rose up to God.
> God heard their groaning, and he remembered his covenant promise to Abraham, Isaac, and Jacob.
> He looked down on the people of Israel and knew it was time to act."
> (Exodus 2:23)

In Exodus 3, God comes to Mt. Sinai and proclaims to Moses, who is now an adult, "I have seen… I have heard… I am aware… I have come." All of this must have sounded pretty good to Moses, but then it got personal. What did God say His plan was for rescuing His people? (Exodus 3:7-10)

We know God could do it all on His own. He is Omnipotent, which means all-powerful. Yet, in today's study we have seen He used Shiphrah, Puah, Moses' mother, Moses' sister, and now Moses himself.

Why do you think God involves people in His work?

What question did Moses ask when he heard God's plan? (Notice he asked the same thing twice!) (Exodus 3:11)

_____

In Vs. 12, God answered beginning with these words:

_____

So the real question wasn't "Who is Moses?" but "Who is *with* Moses?" And the same is true of us.

Who is this one who is *with* us? What are some things you know to be true about God?

In Vs. 14-15 God answers the question "Who will be with Moses?" What insight does God give?

GOD
WORLD
MAN
WOMAN

Kingdom of God **PATTERN**

FALL
FLOOD
TOWER OF BABEL

Kingdom of God **PERISHED**

ABRAM *(ABRAHAM)*
ISHMAEL
ISAAC
JACOB *(ISRAEL)*
JOSEPH
13. MOSES

Kingdom of God **PROMISED**

41

Lesson Eight

In Exodus 4 the Lord sought to give Moses a fresh glimpse into who He is. God performed three miraculous signs as Moses watched. The Lord took some <u>familiar</u> things (Moses' staff, his hand, and some water), things which Moses knew well, and turned them into something <u>new</u>. God initiates. God changes things. Even things we think we know the substance of. Even things we don't expect anything different from. (Read Exodus 4:1-12 to see how this scene unfolded.)

GOD HAD JUST DONE SOMETHING <u>NEW</u> WITH SOMETHING <u>FAMILIAR</u>!

Moses should have expected that God could do the same with him. Nevertheless, throughout his life Moses would be continually plagued with how extensive his shortcomings were, and how enormous the task seemed. In Exodus 4 he continues to argue his case with the Lord.

In Exodus 4:10, what was Moses focused on?

Moses was still unconvinced, so God made a concession for him and allowed Moses' brother Aaron to partner with him. God will tell Moses, Moses will tell Aaron, and Aaron will tell the people. This was only a second-best plan, and eventually Moses would find out that he would have been better off not involving Aaron in the first place. Let's not settle for second-best in *our* lives! When God calls us, let's trust that "the **One** who calls you is faithful and **He** will do it." (I Thes. 5:24) We don't need to look around for someone who appears to be more qualified.

PRAYER MOMENT

Often, God's assignment for us looks way too big to handle. It is then that we must embrace and rely on God's all-sufficient power to carry it out through us. As God showed Moses, He is able to do something new with something familiar (with you!). Below, in prayer, list the things that look too big in your life right now under the "Who am I?" column. Then next to them, write what you know to be true about God that makes Him qualified to handle these things under the "Who is **WITH** me?" column.

WHO AM I?	*WHO IS **WITH** ME?*
_____	_____
_____	_____
_____	_____
_____	_____

☐ *Check here when you have filled out your timeline with the new entry from this lesson.*

LESSON NINE

PRAYER MOMENT

"You are my refuge and my shield; Your word is my source of hope." (Psalm 119:114)
Pray, as you begin today, that you will thoroughly understand how God is your **refuge** and your **shield** and that His Word will bring you **hope**.

Over the 430 years that the Israelites inhabited Egypt, they had gone from being harmless visitors, to threatening immigrants, to tolerated slaves, to despised foreigners. Strategically, God sent ten torturous plagues to convince Egypt that it was time for the Israelites to leave. In fact, the Egyptians were so convinced that they gave the Israelites gold, silver, and valuables to further urge Israel to get going. And, although it looked like it would then be smooth sailing for Israel, it did not turn out to be that easy.

BIBLE PASSAGE

Read Exodus 13:17-14:31 and use the space below to record any questions it brings to mind or things you notice.

Israel moved out from Egypt as a mass of slaves set free. Exodus 12:37-38 tells us, "There were about 600,000 men, plus all the women and children. A rabble of non-Israelites went with them." What a crowd to move through the desert. And this was their first taste of freedom in hundreds of years. Let's investigate how God led them…

Exodus 13:17:   God did not _____.

Exodus 13:18:   Instead, God _____.

What was God's reason for leading them the way he did?

Lesson Nine

Do you ever feel, like Israel must have felt, that God is leading you in a round-about way, rather than taking the direct route along the main road? What might be His reason for doing this in your life?

Throughout this journey, what did God use to lead them? (Exodus 13:21-22) Draw here what your imagination pictures when you read this.

At this time the Lord used the pillar of fire and the pillar of cloud to lead His people. Amazing, isn't it? Makes us wish for that kind of leading in our own lives. What are God's tools for leading His people today?

A well-established agenda was at work behind the specific path God had the Israelites on. He was working to accomplish something that had not yet occurred in the hearts of the people. As the path took another round-about turn for the Israelites, the Lord accomplished another facet of his strategy.

What does Exodus 14:3-4 add about God's strategy?

Is all this just another miracle for Israel to remember? Look carefully. Notice that all of what is about to happen is for the *Egyptians* to witness a display of God's glory and to know "I am the LORD." How does He do this? He does this through circumstances Israel cannot handle without Him - clearly, they are powerless to save themselves.

And the same is true for us. Impossible circumstances in our own lives display God's glory to a watching world and convey to them about God: "I am the LORD."

Write here the name of someone who you hope sees God's greatness revealed through your life:

Pharaoh had asked the right question way back when Moses had first spoken to him in Exodus 5:2. What did he ask?

Since it was the right question, God was in the process of answering it before his very eyes. It is a question everyone must grapple with. It is a question *you* must find the answer to as well. Thankfully, the Lord has equipped us with an entire book so we can come to know Him.

Before the Lord had begun this deliverance, He had told Israel that His name would be magnified (He would be seen for who He is) through their deliverance. Read the passages below aloud, if possible, (Exodus 6:2, 3, 5-8, 14:4, 18) and circle the words "I am the LORD."

> And God said to Moses, "I am Yahweh— 'the LORD.' I appeared to Abraham, to Isaac, and to Jacob as El-Shaddai— 'God Almighty'—but I did not reveal my name, Yahweh, to them. You can be sure that I have heard the groans of the people of Israel, who are now slaves to the Egyptians. And I am well aware of my covenant with them…

> "Therefore, say to the people of Israel: 'I am the LORD. I will free you from your oppression and will rescue you from your slavery in Egypt. I will redeem you with a powerful arm and great acts of judgment. I will claim you as my own people, and I will be your God. Then you will know that I am the LORD your God who has freed you from your oppression in Egypt. I will bring you into the land I swore to give to Abraham, Isaac, and Jacob. I will give it to you as your very own possession. I am the LORD!'"

> And once again I will harden Pharaoh's heart, and he will chase after you. I have planned this in order to display my glory through Pharaoh and his whole army. After this the Egyptians will know that I am the LORD!" So the Israelites camped there as they were told…

> "When my glory is displayed through them, all Egypt will see my glory and know that I am the LORD!"

The Lord was at work to display His glory, but Israel could only see one thing. Sum up their response to the opposition they were facing as they spoke in Exodus 14:10-12.

Amazing, isn't it – they looked back on their bondage fondly. They didn't believe freedom would be better. Freedom looked too hard.

Exodus 14:13-14 contains Moses' instructions for Israel for the battle they were facing. Sort out the specifics of the battle plan below:

Israel's part:	God's part:

The Lord Himself adds more information about the plan in vs. 15-17. Continue with the above columns and list these details.

Lesson Nine

Only God could do His part. But the Israelites had a role to play as well, albeit small. Moses would initiate the deliverance by holding his **staff** in his **hand** over the **water**. Underline those key words here:

Vs. 16 - "Pick up your staff and raise your hand over the sea. Divide the water so the Israelites can walk through the middle of the sea on dry ground."

Vs. 21 – "Then Moses raised his hand over the sea, and the lord opened up a path through the water with a strong east wind. The wind blew all that night, turning the seabed into dry land."

Now think back to Lesson Eight. What things had God used to show signs of His miracle-working power to Moses? Glance over Exodus 4:1-9 to refresh your memory.

What lesson was Moses supposed to glean through these signs? (See pg. 42 to remember.)

GOD HAD JUST DONE SOMETHING _____ WITH SOMETHING _____!

This lesson was now unfolding before his eyes and was to be engraved in his memory.

For all time, Israel would remember this miracle. They had been marked as God's people and had been freed from the clutches of the powerful nation of Egypt. It was an experience Egypt would remember too.

Let's sum this all up. The freedom the Lord was accomplishing for the Israelites had a two-fold purpose:

For the Israelites: For the Egyptians:

PRAYER MOMENT

We have seen today that God wants to be seen and known not only by those who are His, but by those outside of the faith as well. He orchestrates and allows things in the lives of His children so unbelievers will know His greatness. Later in the Bible, Nehemiah sums up this point in Israel's history by saying,

"You sent miraculous signs and wonders against Pharaoh, against all his officials and all the people of his land… You made a name for Yourself which remains to this day." (Nehemiah 9:10 NIV)

Take some time to pray for those people in your life you identified earlier in this lesson, those who you want to see God's name (His character and His glory) being displayed through your life. Realize that God is delivering you from your areas of bondage so they may one day be free too.

☐ *Check here when you have filled out your timeline with the new entries from this lesson.*

LESSON TEN

PRAYER MOMENT

How do you personally respond to authority in your life? Talk with God in prayer about this as you begin your study today. Then ask God to teach you from His Word as you open your Bible.

Whew! Did you breathe a sigh of relief when Israel finally came out from under Egypt's oppressive rule? They were now a distinct **people** again and were moving towards God's **place** for them. You'll see that they came under His **rule** in a new and tangible way in the reading before you today. The **blessing** of God's kingdom plan is continuing as the story unfolds.

BIBLE PASSAGE

Read Exodus 19:16-20:21 and use the space below to record any questions it brings to mind or things you notice.

You will find as you study the Bible that the titles given to various sections of Scripture can be quite helpful. Understand that these were not included in the original writings, but contemporary editors have added them in to help us follow the storyline.

Notice the title that precedes today's reading of chapter 19, and write it below:

Let's begin our examination of this section by considering <u>where</u> these events were occurring. We have previously been to this same location once before in our study. It might not ring a bell at first, so look back to Exodus 3.

In Exodus 3:1, what is this same location called?

This is an important place to the Lord. Skim the verses which follow in Exodus 3 to recall the significant event which happened at this mountain at that time.

Lesson Ten

You know how this feels, don't you? When your life comes full circle, and you end up back at a location that held great significance to you? It causes you to reflect, to think about what a different person you are now, and to remember all you have learned in the years that have passed. For Moses, it is quite possible that decades had passed since he was initially called to lead the Israelites here at Mt. Sinai.

What does Moses now know about God? What has he learned in the years since he first heard the name "Yahweh?"

Realize that all of this was on Moses' mind. What sign had God given to Moses at the initial encounter in Exodus 3:12, which explains why God had brought them here once again?

Now we are ready to understand the context for today's reading: God has taken the Israelites out of a place of slavery, marked them as His own people, and brought them to His mountain to teach them how to worship Him.

When you hear the word "worship" what does that mean to you? What do you think worship is?

The word "worship" was originally "worth-ship." It is a declaration that God is worthy to be praised and to be served and to be exalted.

Through a two-step process, the Lord will teach the Israelite people how to worship Him:

Step 1 – Impress upon them His holiness (Chapter 19)

Step 2 – Give them the law which will be a framework of how they can worship Him and live as His holy people (Chapter 20)

The people were enthusiastic about what the Lord was preparing to do in Exodus 19:8. Write what they say below:

Preparation of the people was to precede God's provision of the law. Read Exodus 19:10-15.

What were they to do?

How would this prepare them?

48 Finding Your Way

Verses 16-23 of Exodus 19 paint a vivid picture of what it looked and felt like when God arrived ready to give the law to the people. Draw here what your mind's eye sees as the details unfold in these verses: (I've given you a mountain to start with...)

Why do you think the Lord had them prepare in the way that He did?

Now let's turn to Exodus 20 and examine the Ten Commandments that the Lord gave on that day...

	Summary of Command	Reason for command (if given)
#1 (Vs. 3)		
#2 (Vs. 4-6)		
#3 (Vs. 7)		
#4 (Vs. 8-11)		
#5 (Vs. 12)		
#6 (Vs. 13)		
#7 (Vs. 14)		
#8 (Vs. 15)		
#9 (Vs. 16)		
#10 (Vs. 17)		

Do you see any way these commands could be separated into two groups? *If so, mark that on your list above, and provide subtitles for each section.*

GOD
WORLD
MAN
WOMAN

Kingdom of God
PATTERN

FALL
FLOOD
TOWER OF BABEL

Kingdom of God
PERISHED

ABRAM *(ABRAHAM)*
ISHMAEL
ISAAC
JACOB *(ISRAEL)*
JOSEPH
MOSES
FREE FROM EGYPT
RED SEA
16. EXODUS FROM EGYPT
17. TEN COMMAND-MENTS

Kingdom of God
PROMISED

Lesson Ten

Many years later, Jesus was asked which of the commandments was the most important. As you look at your list above, what do you think He answered?

Now let's find out what His answer was. Read Matthew 22:34-40 and summarize His answer here:

Never were the 10 Commandments intended to make the people good enough to be chosen by God. Remember, these commands are given *after* He had redeemed them from Egypt and had claimed them as His own. Not based on any merit of their own, they are His because He has rescued them.

The law isn't for them to *become* His people, but because they *are* His people.

Through their miraculous escape from Egypt, the Spirit of God had led the Israelites out of bondage and into freedom. So, outwardly, they were free. But inwardly, they were still in slavery to sin.

What would it look like for them to live in freedom on the inside? What are these commands freeing them from?

God had drawn the Israelites out from the rest of the world to make them a people who would represent and reflect Him to the world. God is holy (set apart); therefore, they must be holy. So, He speaks to the greatest areas of temptation for mankind when He lists these 10 commandments.

And it is the same with us. He knows our weaknesses, and He knows what it will take to set us apart from the world so that we can look like Him.

Which commandment speaks to a specific weakness in your life that you grapple with?

PRAYER MOMENT

Jesus later expanded the understanding of the Ten Commandments with His teaching in the Sermon on the Mount (Matthew 5:21a, 22, 27-28):

"You have heard that our ancestors were told," You must not murder…"
But I say, if you are even angry with someone, you are subject to judgment!"

"You have heard the commandment that says, "You must not commit adultery." But I say, anyone who even looks at a woman with lust has already committed adultery with her in his heart."

As you can see, the commandments go beyond the actual acting-out of the sin to also include the heart attitude that precedes the action. With this in mind, pray through the list of the commandments you made on page 37, asking God to keep you from sin in your **actions** and in your **attitudes**.

☐ *Check here when you have filled out your timeline with the new entries from this lesson.*

LESSON ELEVEN

PRAYER MOMENT

Are you more of a leader or a follower? Think that through and pray about what it means for you to keep in step with God as you open your study today.

Before moving into our main passage for today, let's not miss where the book of Exodus ends – with God drawing near to His people. An amazing offer! But the people would have to follow His instructions down to the last detail in preparing this dwelling place. Look at the following Scripture, imagining it as you read, and noticing all that was involved in preparing this tent for the Lord.

> Then the LORD said to Moses, "Set up the Tabernacle on the first day of the new year. Place the Ark of the Covenant inside, and install the inner curtain to enclose the Ark within the Most Holy Place. Then bring in the table, and arrange the utensils on it. And bring in the lampstand, and set up the lamps.
>
> "Place the gold incense altar in front of the Ark of the Covenant. Then hang the curtain at the entrance of the Tabernacle. Place the altar of burnt offering in front of the Tabernacle entrance. Set the washbasin between the Tabernacle and the altar, and fill it with water. Then set up the courtyard around the outside of the tent, and hang the curtain for the courtyard entrance.
>
> "Take the anointing oil and anoint the Tabernacle and all its furnishings to consecrate them and make them holy. Anoint the altar of burnt offering and its utensils to consecrate them. Then the altar will become absolutely holy. Next anoint the washbasin and its stand to consecrate them...
>
> Moses proceeded to do everything just as the LORD had commanded him... He took the stone tablets inscribed with the terms of the covenant and placed them inside the Ark. Then he attached the carrying poles to the Ark, and he set the Ark's cover—the place of atonement—on top of it. Then he brought the Ark of the Covenant into the Tabernacle and hung the inner curtain to shield it from view, just as the LORD had commanded him.
>
> Next Moses placed the table in the Tabernacle, along the north side of the Holy Place, just outside the inner curtain. And he arranged the Bread of the Presence on the table before the lord, just as the LORD had commanded him.
>
> He set the lampstand in the Tabernacle across from the table on the south side of the Holy Place. Then he lit the lamps in the LORD's presence, just as the LORD had commanded him. He also placed the gold incense altar in the Tabernacle, in the Holy Place in front of the inner curtain. On it he burned the fragrant incense, just as the LORD had commanded him.
>
> He hung the curtain at the entrance of the Tabernacle, and he placed the altar of burnt offering near the Tabernacle entrance. On it he offered a burnt offering and a grain offering, just as the LORD had commanded him.
>
> Next Moses placed the washbasin between the Tabernacle and the altar. He filled it with water so the priests could wash themselves. Moses and Aaron and Aaron's sons used water from it to wash their hands and feet. Whenever they approached the altar and entered the Tabernacle, they washed themselves, just as the LORD had commanded Moses.
>
> Then he hung the curtains forming the courtyard around the Tabernacle and the altar. And he set up the curtain at the entrance of the courtyard. So at last Moses finished the work. (Exodus 40:1-33)

Did you notice the many details that were involved in preparing this place for the Lord? Skim back over the above passage and circle each of the items which had been made and put into place (such as the Ark of the Covenant, the inner curtain). *Do an online search of "Tabernacle" if you'd like to see what all of this looked like when it was put in place.*

All these items were actually visual aids to instruct the people in how to relate to the holy God who had come to dwell in their midst. Relating to the Lord in this way was a unique blessing that the Israelites alone were given.

Lesson Eleven

What recurring phrase did you notice as you read the above passage?

"_____ as the _____ had _____."

The Israelites would have to come to God *on His terms*, *in His way*, just as we must do today:

- They came to God through His provision of the Tabernacle.
- We come to God through the provision of His Son Jesus – the "new and living way." (Hebrews 10:20)

BIBLE PASSAGE

Read Numbers 9:1-23 and use the space below to record any questions it brings to mind or things you notice.

Looking back and remembering... that is what Numbers 9:1-14 is about. What is it they were to remember? (See also Exodus 12:1-16, 28-33 for more detail.)

Is there a story of deliverance in your life that you want to remember? From what has God delivered you or your family line? When you look back on this, what does it make you feel? What does it show you about God?

Looking forward and following... that is what Numbers 9:15-23 is about. What did this look like for the Israelites?

When the cloud moved, they moved – it looks so simple as we read it. But it did require that they respond in obedience. Did they ever resist, I wonder? Were there ever some who refused to move? Perhaps some stayed behind when the cloud moved on because they had settled quite nicely in this place, thank you very much. Surely some moved on resentfully. This must have felt tedious – all this uprooting and packing, then settling in and unpacking again for who knows how long – a day? a year? "Why, Lord?" Surely there must have been a point to this exercise.

Spend some time in prayer and explore that with the Lord. What *was* the point of this exercise? List here everything you think of:

Granted, the Lord's leading in our lives looks much different than it did in theirs. But we are asked to respond by following just as they were. Reflect on the list you made above. **Which of these things is the Lord trying to accomplish in your life right now, as He calls you to follow Him? Put a star by any that apply to you.**

PRAYER MOMENT

Verse 23 (NLT) ends this chapter declaring: "So they camped or traveled

_____ and they did _____

_____ told them…"

Write verse 23 below in your own words, as a prayer to the Lord:

☐ *Check here when you have filled out your timeline with the new entries from this lesson.*

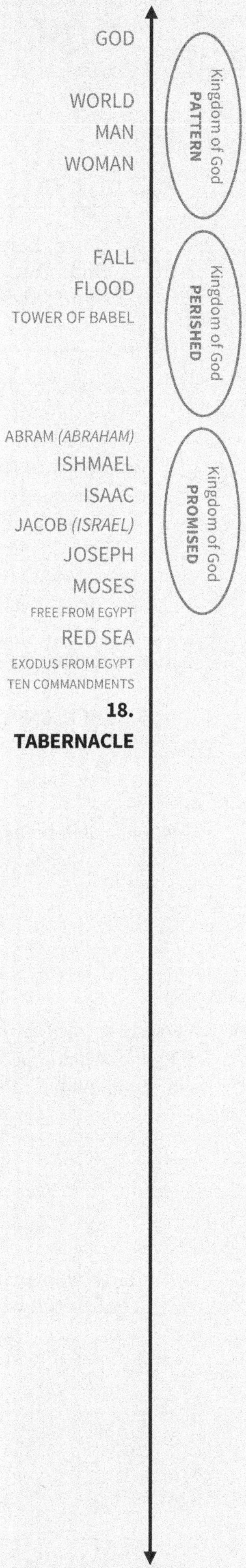

Timeline (right margin):

Kingdom of God — PATTERN
- GOD
- WORLD
- MAN
- WOMAN

Kingdom of God — PERISHED
- FALL
- FLOOD
- TOWER OF BABEL

Kingdom of God — PROMISED
- ABRAM *(ABRAHAM)*
- ISHMAEL
- ISAAC
- JACOB *(ISRAEL)*
- JOSEPH
- MOSES
- FREE FROM EGYPT
- RED SEA
- EXODUS FROM EGYPT
- TEN COMMANDMENTS
- **18. TABERNACLE**

53

LESSON TWELVE

> ## PRAYER MOMENT
>
> "Lord, help me not to fear, for You are with me. Help me not be afraid, for you are my God. You will strengthen me, and help me, and hold me up by your righteous right hand." (Isaiah 41:10 paraphrase)

It looked ominous, threatening and impossible. Despite all the anticipation that had preceded this moment, they felt dread, not joy, as they contemplated what was before them. Have you ever had a moment that felt like this? Well, the Israelites were paralyzed with fear when they peered into the land God promised to them. They anticipated what it would take to inhabit it for themselves, and concluded, "This was not what we signed up for when we left the oppression of Egypt."

Because of their fear, Israelite spies were sent to scout out the land. Surprisingly, they returned with conflicting reports.

Summarize what ensued when the spies returned.

Response of 10 Spies (Numbers 13:25-28):

Response of 2 Spies (Numbers 14:6-9):

Response of People (Numbers 14:1-4):

Response of the Lord (Numbers 14:21-30, 34):

Verse 22 says, *"They have seen my glorious presence and the miraculous signs I performed…"* Glance back over your timeline. What impossible situations had the Lord overcome for the Israelites in the past? How should those have equipped them for this current situation?

This was just a ***different kind of impossible***. This is true for us as well. When we are confronted with a different kind of impossible, we <u>must</u> remember our history with God.

Take a moment to pray about this for yourself, detailing any impossible situations you are currently grappling with.

54   Finding Your Way

Lesson Twelve

God was fully capable of delivering the land to them, but the Israelites missed this blessing because their fear was greater than their faith. As a result, God prohibited this generation from entering the land. Instead, they would be subjected to forty years of wandering in the desert. They had forfeited God's gracious provision because of a lack of faith. May that never be said of us.

Although this wasn't God's original plan for the Israelites, He was still faithful. Underline below all the ways God extended His grace to His chosen people during their forty years of desert wanderings.

"Because of your great compassion you did not abandon them in the wilderness. By day the pillar of cloud did not fail to guide them on their path, nor the pillar of fire by night to shine on the way they were to take. You gave your good Spirit to instruct them. You did not withhold your manna from their mouths, and you gave them water for their thirst. For forty years you sustained them in the wilderness; they lacked nothing, their clothes did not wear out nor did their feet become swollen.
(Nehemiah 9:19-21)

What a picture of God's commitment to His people!

Now we are caught up to the point where today's Bible passage comes in. We will have only one reading from the book of Joshua. But it is a key event - one by which you'll want to remember this book of the Bible.

BIBLE PASSAGE

Read Joshua 5:13-6:27 and use the space below to record any questions it brings to mind or things you notice.

Notice that just before this scene opens, in Joshua 5:10, Israel is celebrating the Passover again. Forty years have passed, and the people are still looking back on that event! What was this celebration causing them to recall?

Read Joshua 5:13-15. What a stunning encounter this is! Many interpreters believe this is a "Christophany," an appearance of Jesus Christ which occurred before His birth.

When Joshua is faced with this imposing character, he asks a question in verse 13. Write his question below:

Kingdom of God Promised 55

Lesson Twelve

Other versions of the Bible phrase the question in this way: "Are you for us or against us?" Joshua knew he was in unfriendly territory, so this was a natural question. However, it appears to be the wrong question. Why?

Joshua asks the right question in verse 14. Write his question here:

So, the proper question isn't, "Is God for or against me?" but, "Am *I* for or against *Him*?" Am I partnering with Him in the midst of what He is doing? Or am I surging ahead and expecting God to follow where I want to go? When I acknowledge that God is the commander and I am the servant, I ask, "What do you want me to do?" This is what it means to be under the Lord's rule, following Him as the leader and director. And Joshua himself is about to learn more about following the Lord…

To be sure, the battle plans sound strange as we read them at the beginning of Joshua 6. But notice two things:

How will the city be at first? (Vs. 1)   How will the city be at the end? (Vs. 5)

Instructions were given to the Israelites about what must be destroyed and what must be kept when they entered the city. Read vs. 17-19, and outline below what details are given.

It sounds harsh to us when we read this battle plan. Everything must be "completely destroyed," except what can be used in worship in the Tabernacle. **Understand that the most threatening disease that would plague Israel throughout their history was conformity** (the inclination to be the *same* as the culture surrounding them). Over and over, throughout their history, the Israelites would be inclined to choose *sameness* over *holiness*. They would try to meld their faith with the idolatry around them. Knowing their tendency to this weakness, the Lord instructs them to eradicate every vestige of the culture which they were dethroning here.

In this scene we see God sovereignly extending grace to the Israelites, while at the same time exercising justice with the Canaanites. The people of Jericho were indeed wicked pagan people, but the Israelites were not without sin themselves. God, in His sovereign authority, chose to give the Israelites His grace, so He could build through them a new nation, a holy people set apart for Him.

Before we leave the book of Joshua, we'll look at the closing scene in Joshua 24. As you read this chapter, remember the events on your timeline and all we have been through with Israel. Now read Joshua 24:1-13.

In light of the path the people have walked with God, Joshua issues a challenge in Joshua 24:14-15. Sum it up below.

Finish by reading verses 16-28. Joshua had committed to following the Lord and He yearned to see the people do the same. But he says in verse 19, *"You are not able to serve the Lord, for God is holy."* Yes, we too are in desperate need of God's grace if we are to follow and serve Him. To be sure, we will fail time and time again, but this brings us to a realization of our need for the One who alone lived perfectly – Jesus Christ.

PRAYER MOMENT

The same challenge faces you which faced Israel that day: Have you committed your life to God, to serve and follow Him? Take some time to think and pray about that now.

☐ *Check here when you have filled out your timeline with the new entry from this lesson.*

GOD
WORLD
MAN
WOMAN

Kingdom of God PATTERN

FALL
FLOOD
TOWER OF BABEL

Kingdom of God PERISHED

ABRAM *(ABRAHAM)*
ISHMAEL
ISAAC
JACOB *(ISRAEL)*
JOSEPH
MOSES
FREE FROM EGYPT
RED SEA
EXODUS FROM EGYPT
TEN COMMANDMENTS
TABERNACLE
19. WILDERNESS WANDERINGS
20. JOSHUA
21. ENTER PROMISED LAND

Kingdom of God PROMISED

KINGDOM OF GOD
PARTIAL

LESSON THIRTEEN

What is it about us that drives us to perpetually test the boundaries? If there's a rule, we want to push back and see if we can get around it. One of my kids demonstrated this when he was only three. Interrupting a quiet evening, I heard a blood curdling scream come from upstairs. I dashed up, only to find him crying on the bed next to our cat. Immediately I knew what had happened. "Don't try to pet Fat Kitty – she's grumpy," we had told him time and again. This cat was terribly afraid of little kids and didn't respond well to their friendliness. That night, this three-year-old snuck upstairs and decided to check the validity of our rule. Suffice it to say, he didn't have to check that rule again.

Can you remember a time when you decided to test a rule as a child and incurred a consequence?

PRAYER MOMENT

Are you a rule-keeper or rule-bender? How does this translate into your relationship with God? Consider this in prayer as you open this lesson today.

BIBLE PASSAGE

Read Judges 2:1-23 and use the space below to record any questions it brings to mind or things you notice.

This chapter begins with a summary statement about a problem that would repeatedly surface in the book of Judges.

In verse 2, what had the Israelites been told to do? And what did they do in response to God's instruction?

So, the Israelites allowed the false gods of foreign nations to remain in their land; these would be a constant temptation to them. Let's look at the scene that follows in Judges 2 to see how this would play out.

Kingdom of God Partial

Lesson Thirteen

Outline the progression of events which unfolds in verses 11-19.

Circle and label these elements in the progression you've outlined above:

<u>S</u>in
<u>W</u>orship of false gods
<u>O</u>ppression
<u>R</u>epentance
<u>D</u>eliverance

This acronym, S.W.O.R.D., illustrates the cycle which the Israelites found themselves repeating in the book of Judges. Since they refused to follow God's instruction, they would repeatedly find it necessary to take up the sword to get out from under the consequences of the Lord's discipline.

Place the words from the S.W.O.R.D. acronym into the diagram below.

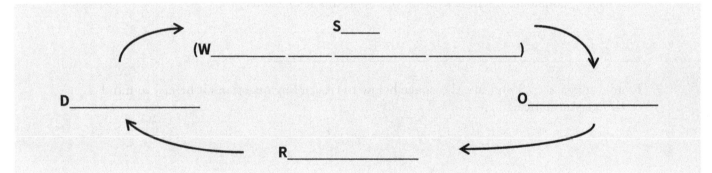

This cycle is repeated a dozen times in the book of Judges. Let's take a look at one more scene to see this illustrated again.

Read Judges 3:7-11 and as you read, diagram the S.W.O.R.D. facets of this story below.

It's easy to observe the foolishness of the Israelites as we look at this repeated cycle. Are you willing to see that the same progression unfolds in your own life sometimes? Give some honest thought to the following questions.

Sin...Worship: What sin have you recently fallen into, determining that this was more important than honoring God with your obedience? What are you worshipping when you fall prey to this sin?

Oppression: Have you found yourself stuck there, suffering the consequences? What is that experience like?

Repentance: Will you repent of that sin by expressing your regret to God and asking for His forgiveness? Why or why not?

Deliverance: Did God provide deliverance for you? Or did He give you steps you need to take to get out from under that sin?

When we see how the Lord persevered with the Israelites, repeatedly forgiving and delivering them as they cried out, it can give us hope that He will stick with us too. In grace, God continues because...

"He is patient with you, not wanting anyone to perish, but everyone to come to repentance." (II Peter 3:9)

PRAYER MOMENT

Don't miss the fact that the Israelites' rescue always involved God providing a deliverer, in the form of a judge, to help them shake free from the consequences of their sin. It is the same for us. Our Deliverer, Jesus, comes to set us free from the sin that entangles and oppresses us. What hope that brings!

Take a moment to pray about where you are in your sin struggle, asking Jesus to bring deliverance to you there.

☐ *Check here when you have filled out your timeline with the new entry from this lesson.*

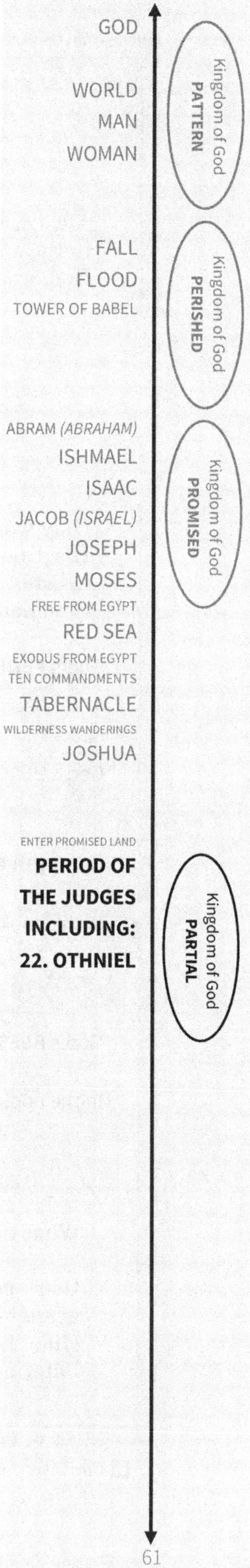

Timeline (sidebar):

- GOD
- WORLD
- MAN
- WOMAN

Kingdom of God: PATTERN

- FALL
- FLOOD
- TOWER OF BABEL

Kingdom of God: PERISHED

- ABRAM (ABRAHAM)
- ISHMAEL
- ISAAC
- JACOB (ISRAEL)
- JOSEPH
- MOSES
- FREE FROM EGYPT
- RED SEA
- EXODUS FROM EGYPT
- TEN COMMANDMENTS
- TABERNACLE
- WILDERNESS WANDERINGS
- JOSHUA

Kingdom of God: PROMISED

- ENTER PROMISED LAND
- **PERIOD OF THE JUDGES INCLUDING:**
- **22. OTHNIEL**

Kingdom of God: PARTIAL

Lesson Thirteen

BIBLICAL THEME:
THE KINGDOM OF GOD

Always, God's desire was to establish a kingdom which would reflect His goodness to the surrounding nations, drawing them also to Himself. This, the **Kingdom of God**, would involve:

God's _____

in God's _____

under God's _____

enjoying God's _____

Only when the Israelites functioned as God's people, living in His place and under His rule, would they display God's blessing to a watching world. When they insisted on conforming to the culture surrounding them, choosing sameness rather than holiness, they failed to glorify God and they disrupted the plan.

God's **PEOPLE:** Who are God's People here?

God's **PLACE:** Are the people in the place where God intended them to be?

God's **RULE:** How are they doing at following the lead of the King? Are they obeying Him?

In the book of Joshua: In the book of Judges:

God's **BLESSING:** Are the people enjoying God's blessing? How do we see that?

In the book of Joshua: In the book of Judges:

What title would you give this period? **Kingdom of God** _____.

God's people are finally in God's place, the Promised Land. They have His law available to them, but they go in and out of obeying it. When they are following Him they do experience His blessing, but their obedience is intermittent and faltering. We will be calling this period the **"KINGDOM OF GOD PARTIAL."**

☐ *Check here when you have written "Kingdom of God Partial" in Oval D on your Timeline.*

LESSON FOURTEEN

"Samson judged Israel for twenty years during the period when the Philistines dominated the land."
Judges 15:20

PRAYER MOMENT

"Unfulfilled potential" – that's what today's study is about. Pray about whatever is brought to your mind by that phrase.

BIBLE PASSAGE

Read Judges 16:4-31 and use the space below to record any questions it brings to mind or things you notice.

As you read this section you quickly see that Samson is a study in contrasts – a man of ***great strengths***...and of ***great weaknesses***.

Samson's Great Strengths: *these are the qualities God gave him.*

In Judges 14:5-14 Samson outsmarted a group of men with a clever riddle he devised. What type of strength does this reveal in Samson?

What strength is Samson most known for?

How is it demonstrated in the following passages?

Judges 14:5-6   Judges 15:14-16   Judges 16:29-30

Lesson Fourteen

Samson's Great Weaknesses: *this is what he did with what God gave him.*

Look at the following passages and list the women in the story. What do Samson's interactions with these women demonstrate about him?

Judges 14:1-20   Judges 16:1   Judges 16:4-20

What was Samson's motive for tearing down the temple? What does that reveal about his character (Judges 16:28)? We also see a similar motive in his earlier violence against the Philistines (Judges 15:7-8).

Samson was distinguished as a "Nazarite" when he was born. As such, he lived under a commitment to be set apart as consecrated to the Lord. This vow, outlined in Numbers 6, required one to abstain from fermented drink, avoid contact with any dead body and refrain from cutting one's hair.

As we look at Samson's life, we see he disregards this high calling, breaking each part of the oath. What does that tell you about who he is?

Sum up the dichotomy seen in Samson in the space below:

Samson was...

Use your imagination. How could Samson's accomplishments been different if he had lived up to the potential God gifted him with?

By and large, the Judges were a severe disappointment. Samson was a fool, repeatedly chasing immoral women and falling prey to his own ego. Another judge named Jepthah sacrificed his own daughter after making an impulsive vow. Clearly these judges are not godly heroes on a Sunday school coloring page who we should emulate. It is almost amazing that the Lord used such flawed individuals to free his people from the oppression brought about by their own foolishness. As we read about these judges, we are left yearning for a better solution for Israel. And the Israelites felt the same. In fact, four times in the book of Judges this phrase is repeated:

"In those days _____ _____ _____ _____

and ____ _____ _____ did _____ _____ _____ in their

_____ _____."

(Judges 21:25 NLT)

Who is this king they were to long for? How does this tie into the Kingdom of God theme we have been tracking throughout our study?

PRAYER MOMENT

Unfulfilled potential! Samson was used by God in spite of himself. How much more could he have been used by God if he had followed God wholeheartedly? Only a partial and temporary defeat of the Philistines was accomplished through Samson's efforts. We will see that eighty years later the Israelites were still contending with the Philistines when David faced Goliath.

How about you? What strengths has God gifted you with, and what weaknesses do you struggle with? What might be the full potential that God could use you for? With this in mind, write a prayer below:

☐ *Check here when you have filled out your timeline with the new entry from this lesson.*

LESSON FIFTEEN

When we are unaware…before we have even noticed anything…behind the scenes God is at work. We can only see His work when it bursts forth into our daily experience. But this does not mean God has just begun His activity at that moment. So often He has been at work long before, in quietness and secrecy. Preparing things for their perfect timing.

Such is the case in the story we are studying today. In the story before us, we will look at the quiet, behind-the-scenes preparation of Israel's last judge, Samuel. He was just a boy at the time, and at first only a few would know about what had transpired between him and the Lord. However, God was at work preparing him during these formative years, readying him for the role he would play in Israel's history during a time of transition.

PRAYER MOMENT

"Jesus replied, 'My Father is always working, and so am I.'" (John 5:17)

Ponder this verse, and then pray over whatever it causes you to think about.

BIBLE PASSAGE

Read I Samuel 3:1-4:11 and use the space below to record any questions it brings to mind or things you notice.

In I Samuel 3:10 what was Samuel's response to the Lord's voice? What do you think are the key words in that phrase?

In what ways was that the right response to the Lord's voice?

Now let's look at the other things Samuel did in the verses which follow:

	What he did	What character trait this displays
3:18		
3:19		
3:21-4:1		

66 Finding Your Way

Notice how Samuel's obedient and submitted spirit manifested itself in the **words** he spoke. "He told"…"he said"…"his words went out."

What do the following Scriptures tell us about our words?

Proverbs 10:32:   Luke 6:43-45:

"May the words of my mouth and the meditation of my heart be pleasing to you, O Lord, my rock and my redeemer," the Psalmist prays in Psalm 19:14. The mouth and the heart – these two are interconnected.

We have the opportunity to examine a vivid character contrast in these chapters: the contrast between Samuel and the sons of Eli, Hophni and Phinehas. Who are these two guys? And what have they done that so angered the Lord? Well, these young men also worked in the Tabernacle, but their hearts were not tuned to serve the Lord. Rather, they just used that role to indulge themselves.

Turn back to I Samuel and examine Hophni and Phinehas as you did Samuel above.

	What they did	What character trait this displays
2:12-14		
2:22-23		
2:23-25		

The Lord is aware and makes a declaration in I Samuel 2:30:

"I will _____ those who _____, and…

… I will _____ those who _____."

What would God do to carry this out? (I Samuel 2:35)

What would God do to carry this out? (I Samuel 2:31)

(I Samuel 4:11)

We see demonstrated here that the Lord's actions are always consistent with His character. He is righteous, holy and just, and He is not to be trifled with.

GOD
WORLD
MAN
WOMAN

Kingdom of God **PATTERN**

FALL
FLOOD
TOWER OF BABEL

Kingdom of God **PERISHED**

ABRAM *(ABRAHAM)*
ISHMAEL
ISAAC
JACOB *(ISRAEL)*
JOSEPH
MOSES
FREE FROM EGYPT
RED SEA
EXODUS FROM EGYPT
TEN COMMANDMENTS
TABERNACLE
WILDERNESS WANDERINGS
JOSHUA

Kingdom of God **PROMISED**

ENTER PROMISED LAND
PERIOD OF THE JUDGES
INCLUDING:
OTHNIEL
SAMSON
23. JUDGE SAMUEL

Kingdom of God **PARTIAL**

As we read chapter 4, it seems that the nation of Israel had lost sight of this God they were to follow. When they are faced with the Philistines they say,

"If we bring [the Ark of the Covenant] into battle with us it will save us from our enemies." (I Samuel 4:3)

How had their focus shifted?

The Israelites treated the Ark with superstition, believing it to be a good-luck charm. They had seen other nations carry idols into battle, and Israel followed this example. They were trusting the symbol of the covenant rather than the God of the covenant.

It was into this culture that the Lord called Samuel to serve as Israel's last judge. His integrity, his honesty and his ability to hear from the Lord and to accurately relay those messages to the people would be a blessing to the people if they would listen to him. Time would tell.

PRAYER MOMENT

Reflecting back on the contrast between Samuel and Hophni and Phinehas, take some time now to pray for a few of the young people in your life. List their names here:

Go back over today's lesson, noting both the positive and negative character traits we saw in the young men we studied today. Circle each trait as you pray about these qualities for the young people you have listed.

☐ *Check here when you have filled out your timeline with the new entry from this lesson.*

LESSON SIXTEEN

PRAYER MOMENT

"Dear God, Open my heart to learn from both the negative and positive examples I will see in this lesson today."

Complete this phrase: "The grass is always greener _____."

Can you remember a time when you thought this? Briefly explain here:

In the Scriptures leading up to today's Bible passage, the Israelites would experience this for themselves. As we studied Samson in Lesson 14, what did we determine about the Judges in general?

Faced with disappointment after disappointment, the Israelites concluded that the Judges were woefully inadequate to lead Israel. They were yearning for something…but couldn't quite put their finger on it. What *was* it that they needed…

What did they conclude they needed in I Samuel 8:1-5?

What were the reasons for their requesting a king?

What did God tell Samuel to do in I Samuel 8:7?

What did this request for a king represent (Vs. 7-9)?

List the warnings they were given about what life with a king would be like (I Samuel 8:10-19):

With these sobering warnings ringing in their ears, how did Israel proceed (I Samuel 8:19)?

Lesson Sixteen

Verse 20 specifies their reasoning:

"We want _____..."

Here it is again in Israel's history: conformity! The desire for sameness, rather than holiness! What a hold that had on them! Truly it was their Achilles heel.

What angered God is not their request for a king, but their motivation behind that request. See, they wanted a king instead of God, rather than a king under God. The Lord had uniquely designed Israel to be the nation He would personally lead – a theocracy. They chafed under this unique calling, yearning instead for the leading of a human king - a monarchy.

How about you? In what areas in your life do you find it difficult to be different, to be what God is asking you to be?

The Israelites wanted a person instead of God. How about you? Do you look first to certain people to solve your problems or satisfy your needs? Take a moment to talk that through with the Lord in prayer.

Now, the Lord knew all along that this day would come for Israel. In fact, He had given guidelines way back in Deuteronomy about how their appointment of a king should play out.

Using your creativity, on the sketch below represent on the guidelines for a king as detailed in Deuteronomy 17:14-20.

In I Samuel 12 we witness the passing of the baton from Samuel the Judge to Saul the king. Samuel reflected on Israel's history as he spoke to the people that day. Remembering all you have documented on your timeline, read Samuel's farewell address, and reflect on the events he refers to.

So, the Lord accommodated their request by giving them their first king: Saul. The Bible describes him as being wealthy, handsome, and tall. Surely he was well qualified, with all of that going for him! Ha! They insisted on a king at the <u>wrong time</u> and with the <u>wrong motivation</u>. The people had rejected the Lord's leadership over them and they, in turn, got a king who would do the same. When King Saul overtly and repeatedly rejected God's authority, God rejected him as king, and instructed Samuel to anoint a new king.

Turn to I Samuel 16 and read the chapter title to see who this new king is:

_____

Now read I Samuel 16:1-13.

Lesson Sixteen

In a moment, this unsuspecting young shepherd was given a life call. His father and brothers didn't see in him the making of a king. Even Samuel was surprised. Yet this was God's choice. It would take many years, and a circuitous path, for David to be seated on the throne. But in the Lord's eyes David became king that day.

BIBLE PASSAGE

Read I Samuel 17:1-58 and use the space below to record any questions it brings to mind or things you notice.

David has been anointed king, but where was he and what was he doing as the chapter opens? (I Samuel 17:15-18)

What was David's primary concern as he heard Goliath's taunts? (I Samuel 17:26, 45)

Read verses 34-37 again. David knew what he had seen God do for him in the past, and trusted God with this situation too. This was just a different kind of impossible. He knew his God was the same.

Contrast the following:

What Goliath Brought into Battle (I Samuel 17:4-7)	**What David Brought into Battle** (I Samuel 17:40)

David's defeat seemed unavoidable. But he had an unseen Weapon on his side. In verses 45-47 he describes His God in these ways: "The Lord of Heaven's Armies," "The God of the Armies of Israel," "The Conquering Lord," "A God in Israel," "The Rescuing Lord," and "The Battling Lord."

PRAYER MOMENT

In what area of your life are you facing a "Goliath?" Something ominous and impossible and threatening? As you look back over the names of God listed above, pray through each title and ask God to show the same character in your situation as He did with David.

☐ *Check here when you have filled out your timeline with the new entries from this lesson.*

Kingdom of God PATTERN
GOD
WORLD
MAN
WOMAN

Kingdom of God PERISHED
FALL
FLOOD
TOWER OF BABEL

Kingdom of God PROMISED
ABRAM (ABRAHAM)
ISHMAEL
ISAAC
JACOB (ISRAEL)
JOSEPH
MOSES
FREE FROM EGYPT
RED SEA
EXODUS FROM EGYPT
TEN COMMANDMENTS
TABERNACLE
WILDERNESS WANDERINGS
JOSHUA

Kingdom of God PARTIAL
ENTER PROMISED LAND
JUDGES INCLUDING
OTHNIEL
SAMSON
JUDGE SAMUEL
24. ISRAEL INSISTS ON A KING
25. KING SAUL
26. KING DAVID

LESSON SEVENTEEN

PRAYER MOMENT

*"Do not let this Book of the Law depart from your mouth.
Meditate on it day and night so that you may be careful to do everything written in it,
then you will be prosperous and successful."*
Joshua 1:8

Pray now that you would increase in wisdom as you meditate on the Bible today.

Have you ever been faced with a task that you were woefully unequipped for? As the next king of Israel ascended the throne, this was the sense he had. "How on earth can I succeed at the assignment I am facing?"

BIBLE PASSAGE

Read I Kings 3:1-28 and use the space below to record any questions it brings to mind or things you notice.

If we would just listen to what God says, pay attention and remember, we would be prepared in advance for so many things that come our way! Reading God's Word regularly, as you have been doing, is a vital part of being prepared for what life throws at you.

How would Solomon's choices have been different if he had been doing what we prayed above in Joshua 1:8? Specifically, as seen in the opening verses of I Kings 3, what guideline for kings had he disregarded? (Hint: refer back to the previous lesson where you diagrammed what a king must do.)

Verse 3 indicates an additional problem in Solomon's behavior:

"Solomon loved the Lord and followed all the decrees of his father, David, _____

that Solomon, too, offered sacrifices and burned incense at the _____."

The amazing thing here is what unfolds next. God met Solomon at his "except." God came to Solomon in his place of disobedience, invaded it with His holy presence, and made an offer to him there.

72 Finding Your Way

This is **GRACE** – God coming to us in our sin and offering us something better - God opening to us the door to be something beyond our sin and disobedience - God inviting us to turn from life on our own, and to engage with Him. This is grace, greater than all our sin!

What is the question that God poses to Solomon in Vs. 5?

"Ask, and I will give it to you!" With this breathtaking offer before Solomon, what did he ask for?

Let's get more detail on this. What words does Solomon use to describe this wisdom? (Vs. 9)

How does the Lord describe this wisdom? (Vs. 11-12)

Solomon was faced with an overwhelming task when he was given the assignment of leading the people of Israel. In this interaction with the Lord, Solomon sees his shortcoming when he is brought face to face with the One who *is* sufficient.

Again, we are seeing a pattern we have witnessed before as the Lord interacts with man:

SOLOMON SEES HIS NEED → **SOLOMON SEES HIS INABILITY TO MEET HIS NEED** → **GOD MEETS THE NEED**

When you face your insufficiency, you can find that God has the very thing you need. He *is* sufficient – He has what you need for the task that is before you. And, amazingly, He offers it to you.

The question, then, is "what do *you* want?" What do you *really* want? Do you want to continue living in your insufficiency, seeing it as an excuse to struggle through the job at hand? Or will you ask, with open and expectant hands, and receive the equipping that only He can give you for the work He has put before you?

If the Lord would ask, "What do *you* want?" how would you answer? What is it that you need in order to complete the work He has put before you?

Lesson Seventeen

Where was Solomon worshipping in verse 3?

Where was Solomon worshipping in verse 15?

What does this contrast show?

How does Solomon's interaction with the prostitutes (I Kings 3:16-28) demonstrate the "wisdom in governing with justice he had asked God for?

Are you left wondering if God still answers our cries for His help? Perhaps you, like Solomon, find yourself severely lacking the wisdom needed for your assignments in life.

Read James 1:5-6.

How does God respond to your request for wisdom today?

PRAYER MOMENT

Imagine now that God Himself has asked you the question He asked Solomon, "What do you want?" "What do you need for the task before you?" Write your answer below as a prayer to the One who asks.

☐ *Check here when you have filled out your timeline with the new entry from this lesson.*

74 Finding Your Way

LESSON EIGHTEEN

PRAYER MOMENT

Begin your study today by praying a prayer spoken by Solomon in I Kings 8:23, 56-60. To meditate on this Scripture, write these verses word for word below. As you write, think about what Solomon prayed, and consider how you would pray these same things at your specific point in life. Highlight any phrases which are especially meaningful to you.

BIBLE PASSAGE

Read I Kings 7:51-8:21, 54-62 and use the space below to record any questions it brings to mind or things you notice.

What was the occasion that called for Solomon's address to the people that day? What finally happened that they were celebrating? (I Kings 7:51-8:1)

What thoughts or emotions do you imagine this would have stimulated in the people that day?

How did Solomon explain this event in I Kings 8:17-21?

Lesson Eighteen

King Solomon, standing before the entire community of Israel, then prayed the prayer which falls in the middle of his address. The verses you transcribed on the previous page in the prayer moment are taken from this prayer. Read over what you wrote.

What do you sense in Solomon's heart at this important time in Israel's history?

What other concern does Solomon allude to at this time in I Kings 8:24-26?

As we read what is on Solomon's mind, we can hear Solomon's wholehearted devotion to God coming through. Engaged in the work the Lord was doing, Solomon was overjoyed at the honor of building a temple for the Lord. And he yearned to see David's family line continue to rule over Israel as God had promised.

This is perhaps the highest point in Israel's history. Let's revisit our **KINGDOM OF GOD** theme to understand why that is the case:

God's **PEOPLE:** Who are God's People here?

God's **PLACE:** Are the people in the place where God intended them to be?

God's **RULE:** How are they doing at following the lead of the King? Are they obeying Him?

God's **BLESSING:** Are the people enjoying God's blessing? How do we see that?

This is the pinnacle of Old Testament history! God's people are in God's place, under God's rule, and are enjoying God's blessing. It looks as if all the promises have finally come to fruition and the Kingdom of God has come. But it is not to last...

Unfortunately, Solomon would soon be distracted from the priorities of God's work.

Why do you think it is so tempting to be distracted from God's work?

In order to understand what unfolds next in Israel's history, let's look at what enticed Solomon away from wholehearted devotion to the Lord's work.

1 Kings 10:14-21   What drew Solomon away? _____

1 Kings 10:26   What drew Solomon away? _____

1 Kings 11:1-3   What drew Solomon away? _____

1 Kings 11:4-8   What drew Solomon away? _____

We see that what Solomon <u>gathered</u> was what Solomon <u>loved</u>. His heart turned toward these things, and away from the Lord.

Now reflect back on the guidelines for kings which we had diagrammed in Lesson 16. List here any of these issues which Solomon had been warned about ahead of time in the guidelines for kings:

What would be the consequence of Solomon's divided allegiance? Read I Kings 11:9-13.

How quickly Israel went from its brilliant high point to a shadowy depressing valley. What follows in the remainder of I Kings and II Kings can be summarized in three words: ***disobedience, division, decline.***

PRAYER MOMENT

Reflect on Solomon's words in the prayer we opened with today. It's sobering to contemplate that Solomon enthusiastically verbalized his devotion to the Lord, yet he wandered away from God in the decisions and affections of daily life. This is a danger we all face as broken human beings, easily drawn away from the Lord we profess our devotion to.

With this in mind, pray through the words of this hymn as you close today:

> *"Prone to wander, Lord, I feel it.*
> *Prone to leave the God I love.*
> *Take my heart, oh take and seal it.*
> *Seal it for Thy courts above."*

"Come Thou Fount," Robert Robinson, 1758

☐ *Check here when you have filled out your timeline with the new entry from this lesson.*

Timeline (Kingdom of God):

- GOD
- WORLD
- MAN
- WOMAN

Kingdom of God — PATTERN

- FALL
- FLOOD
- TOWER OF BABEL

Kingdom of God — PERISHED

- ABRAM (ABRAHAM)
- ISHMAEL
- ISAAC
- JACOB (ISRAEL)
- JOSEPH
- MOSES
- FREE FROM EGYPT
- RED SEA
- EXODUS FROM EGYPT
- TEN COMMANDMENTS
- TABERNACLE
- WILDERNESS WANDERINGS
- JOSHUA

Kingdom of God — PROMISED

- ENTER PROMISED LAND
- PERIOD OF THE JUDGES INCLUDING:
- OTHNIEL
- SAMSON
- JUDGE SAMUEL
- ISRAEL INSISTS ON A KING
- KING SAUL
- KING DAVID
- KING SOLOMON
- **28. TEMPLE**

Kingdom of God — PARTIAL

KINGDOM OF GOD PROPHESIED

LESSON NINETEEN

PRAYER MOMENT

Pray these words as you begin your study today:

*"Dear Lord, help me to learn from your Word today
as I read about two kings I have probably never heard of before.
Give me insight into my life, as I watch them lead their people.
Let me understand what You are trying to teach me through their lives."*

Division! It is found all around us. Groups, companies, families, marriages. What was once a unified whole is divided and no longer works in harmony. What comes to your memory as you think about division? Where have you experienced this? What caused the fracture?

So often a division causes pain: pain for those involved at the time…pain for those who will follow. Today we will watch as division comes to Israel in a way that would chart their history from that day to this. Our scene opens with the spotlight on Solomon's son, Rehoboam…

BIBLE PASSAGE

Read I Kings 12:1-33 and use the space below to record any questions it brings to mind or things you notice.

Think of a difficult decision you recently had to make. What factors did you consider when making the decision? Whose advice or opinion played into the call you made? Looking back, do you think you exhibited wisdom?

In verses 1-11 Rehoboam had a difficult decision to make right at the beginning of his reign. His father, Solomon, had instituted oppressive taxes, and had drafted laborers from among the Israelites for his extravagant building projects. All the tribes except for the tribe of Judah were groaning under this burdensome weight; Judah had been exempted from both the taxes and service.

Lesson Nineteen

Remember how the Lord had cautioned Israel when they begged Him for a king back in I Samuel 8:10-19? (Glance over that passage if you want to refresh your memory.) Well, all of those warnings had come to fruition at this time, and trouble was brewing. So, Rehoboam sought advice from two groups of people.

Who did Rehoboam ask?	What advice did they give?
Vs. 6-7:	Vs. 6-7:
Vs. 8-11:	Vs. 8-11:

Notice that the older men urged Rehoboam to lead as a <u>servant</u> of his people. Take a look at Matthew 20:25-27 and notice who else called people to lead in this way:

_____

What is the key phrase in these verses?

Circle above the people whose advice Rehoboam followed. Paraphrase the response he gave to the people in verse 14 of I Kings 12:

Fill in the words of Proverbs 12:20 here:
"Walk with the wise and _____;
Associate with fools and _____."

Rehoboam's leadership crumbled as a result of the advice he implemented from his immature friends. What were all the consequences which ensued in I Kings 12:16-20?

Who are the older people in your life who will tell you the hard things?

What truth have you heard from one of them recently that you need to implement?

Because Rehoboam heeded the advice of his foolish friends, the nation of Israel divided. Ten of the tribes defected, following Jeroboam as their king. These tribes retained the name of "Israel," and are also referred to as the Northern Kingdom. Rehoboam maintained his authority over only two tribes, Benjamin and Judah. Those whom King Rehoboam ruled became known as "Judah", the Southern Kingdom, and it is there that David's family line continued on the throne.

Finding Your Way

Using the information in the previous paragraph, fill in this diagram:

NORTHERN KINGDOM

(called "_____")

# of tribes: _____

First ruler: _____

Solomon dies → _____
(Solomon's son)

SOUTHERN KINGDOM

(called "_____")

# of tribes: _____

First ruler: _____

Given how he came to the throne, it is not a surprise that King Jeroboam quickly found he was facing his own leadership challenge. What was the problem? (Vs. 25-27)

How did Jeroboam resolve the problem? (Vs. 28-29)

Is this a good resolution? Why or why not?

REHOBOAM – his leadership had led the people into *division*.
JEROBOAM – his leadership had led the people into *disobedience*.

Let's take a moment and reflect on ourselves. Where is your leadership leading people? Begin by answering this question: Who are you leading?

What are you leading these people toward? If they follow your example, where will they end up? What are you modeling for those who are walking in your footprints?

PRAYER MOMENT

In this lesson we observed two kings who responded poorly to the leadership challenges they faced. On the lines below write your name and a purpose statement for your leadership.

_____'s leadership led people into _____.

Talk this through with the Lord, committing it to Him in prayer.

☐ *Check here when you have filled out your timeline with the new entries from this lesson.*

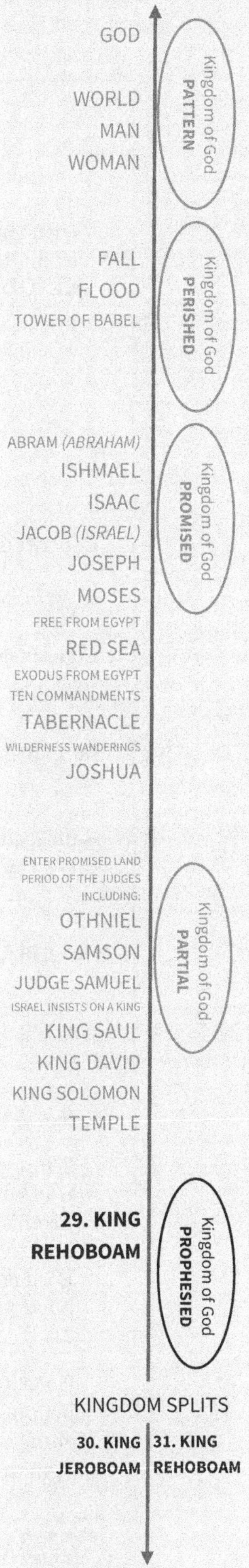

Timeline (right margin):

- GOD
- WORLD
- MAN
- WOMAN

Kingdom of God PATTERN

- FALL
- FLOOD
- TOWER OF BABEL

Kingdom of God PERISHED

- ABRAM (ABRAHAM)
- ISHMAEL
- ISAAC
- JACOB (ISRAEL)
- JOSEPH
- MOSES
- FREE FROM EGYPT
- RED SEA
- EXODUS FROM EGYPT
- TEN COMMANDMENTS
- TABERNACLE
- WILDERNESS WANDERINGS
- JOSHUA

Kingdom of God PROMISED

- ENTER PROMISED LAND
- PERIOD OF THE JUDGES INCLUDING:
- OTHNIEL
- SAMSON
- JUDGE SAMUEL
- ISRAEL INSISTS ON A KING
- KING SAUL
- KING DAVID
- KING SOLOMON
- TEMPLE

Kingdom of God PARTIAL

29. KING REHOBOAM

Kingdom of God PROPHESIED

KINGDOM SPLITS

| 30. KING JEROBOAM | 31. KING REHOBOAM |

Lesson Nineteen

BIBLICAL THEME:
THE KINGDOM OF GOD

With the division of the Northern Kingdom from the Southern Kingdom, we arrive at an important transition in Biblical history. So let's revisit our theme: the **KINGDOM OF GOD**. Remember, that is:

God's _____

in God's _____

under God's _____

enjoying God's _____

God's **PEOPLE:** Who are God's People here?

God's **PLACE:** Are the people in the place where God intended them to be?

God's **RULE:** How are they doing at following the lead of the King? Are they obeying Him?

Is the leadership structure they are under exercising wisdom and leading them into obedience to the Lord?

God's **BLESSING:** Are the people enjoying God's blessing? How do we see that?

As you can see, this is a broken point in Israel's history. Remembering where we've been on our timeline, let's evaluate where we are.

What we called the "**KINGDOM OF GOD PARTIAL**," the partial fulfillment of God's kingdom plan which Israel enjoyed (beginning when they were led into the Promised Land under Joshua) has come to an end. The people are now segmented into two distinct kingdoms. This is a condition which is out of sync with what the Lord declared when He said to Abraham "I will make you into **a great nation**. I will bless you and make you famous and you will be a blessing to others." (Genesis 12:2)

Does God abandon His plan at this point? Enter the prophets to help the people make sense of this, and to provide a glimpse of where this is ultimately going. Since the prophets will be speaking throughout this time, this segment of history can be remembered as the **"KINGDOM OF GOD PROPHESIED."**

☐ *Check here when you have written "Kingdom of God Prophesied" in Oval E on your Timeline.*

LESSON TWENTY

> ## PRAYER MOMENT
>
> *"Look to the Lord and His strength, seek His face always.*
> *Remember the wonders He has done…" (Psalm 105:4-5)*
>
> In prayer, consider the "wonders" the Lord has done for you, and thank Him for these.

Let's pause for a quick review of how we got to this point in Biblical history. In our last lesson we watched as the nation of Israel divided into two distinct nations: Israel in the north and Judah in the south. In the north, King Jeroboam ruled as king. Over the years which followed there would be 19 rulers in the north, all of whom were terrible. The south was first ruled by King Rehoboam. This kingdom did only marginally better than the northern one, having 20 rulers, some of whom were good, throughout its history. The capital city of the Northern Kingdom is Shechem (later called Samaria), and in the south the capital is Jerusalem.

Using the information in the above paragraph, fill in this chart:

LOCATION	NAME OF KINGDOM	# OF RULERS	ANY GOOD RULERS?	CAPITAL CITY
North				( )
South				

Take a few minutes now to commit this chart to memory. You can memorize it by looking at the chart and saying it aloud as you point to each part, "North… South… Israel… Judah… 19… 20," etc. Then try to say it without looking. Trust me, this will be really helpful as you try to follow the history which is about to unfold.

Have you ever explored a cave and been nearly suffocated with the penetrating darkness you experienced there? Strike a single match in that heavy darkness and it will seem to shine with exceptional brilliance.

With the division of Israel into two separate kingdoms, we have entered into a dark time in the history of God's people. The kings in the north and south struggled to lead well and were more often than not a terrible disappointment. But remember who spoke throughout this time? The prophets. These individuals, some bold and some wracked with fear, shone like brilliant flames in the darkness which surrounded them.

A number of the prophets you may have heard of: Isaiah, Jeremiah, Jonah, Elijah. Others are rather obscure characters: Obadiah, Nahum, Habakkuk. But their message is the same and can be summed up in one Hebrew word: shuv. "Turn!" they say. Inherent in this word is the message, "Turn <u>from</u> and turn <u>toward</u>." Now let's read today's passage to understand what the first prophet during this time was urging God's people to turn from, and to turn toward.

Lesson Twenty

BIBLE PASSAGE

Read I Kings 16:29-17:24 and use the space below to record any questions it brings to mind or things you notice.

Refer again to the chart you made on the previous page. As we are studying King Ahab in today's reading, which kingdom are we following? (I Kings 16:29) Circle it below.

Northern Kingdom (Israel) or **Southern Kingdom (Judah)**

In our study, we will first follow the events of the Northern Kingdom, and then we will go back and study the history of the Southern Kingdom.

Looking again at the chart you created on the previous page, how many good kings can we anticipate we will find here in the Northern Kingdom? _____

What distinction had King Ahab earned for himself, according to I Kings 16:31 & 33? Why?

This god, Baal, whom Ahab had turned his people toward, was known as "the giver of rain." But what was going on in chapter 17:1 and 7?

Read **I Kings 17:1-7** and ponder the miracle which unfolds here. Pause long enough to soak it in.

What do you picture? What thoughts and questions does this provoke in you?

Why do you think God took Elijah through this strange experience?

Write below the life lesson Elijah was to cling to from this experience, and then draw a box around this truth:

THE LORD...

Read **I Kings 17:8-16** and answer the same questions.

What do you picture? What thoughts and questions does this provoke in you?

Why do you think God took Elijah through this strange experience?

Write below the life lesson Elijah was to cling to from this experience, and then draw a box around this truth:

THE LORD…

Read **I Kings 17:17-24** and again answer these questions.

What do you picture? What thoughts and questions does this provoke in you?

Why do you think God took Elijah through this strange experience?

Write below the life lesson Elijah was to cling to from this experience, and then draw a box around this truth:

THE LORD…

Time passed and the nation continued to struggle under the drought, and God calls Elijah to speak to the wicked King Ahab. Read **I Kings 18:16-38**.

Sum up what occurred in these verses:

What line was Elijah trying to draw in Vs. 21?

Lesson Twenty

Summarize what the fire miracle was to convey to the people (Vs. 36-37):

Did the people get it (Vs. 39)?

Now reflect on the message of the prophets: "shuv" – "Turn from and turn toward." In what way was that Elijah's message?

How did the lessons Elijah learned in his previous experiences prepare him for the most intimidating experience would face: confronting the wicked King Ahab? (Look back over the points you put a box around.)

PRAYER MOMENT

How about you? What has God been teaching you about Himself recently through your life experiences?

In the last month?
The LORD ...

Over the last year?
The LORD ...

Now pray about what you are currently facing and ask God to increase your faith for this circumstance based on what He has taught you in the past.

☐ *Check here when you have filled out your timeline with the new entries from this lesson.*

LESSON TWENTY-ONE

PRAYER MOMENT

Pray that you will see these truths about God in the book of Jonah today:

"…You are a <u>merciful</u> and <u>compassionate</u> God, slow to get angry and <u>filled with unfailing love</u>. You are <u>eager to turn back from destroying people</u>." (Jonah 4:2b)

Sin…mercy…grace. These are terms which are used freely in Christian circles. But it's easy to let them pass us by, to feel we have a general understanding of what they mean without ever examining them deeply.

What is your understanding of these terms? How would you define them?

SIN:

MERCY:

GRACE:

Beyond just understanding these words, what is your understanding of how these affect you personally? Go back and add that to your definitions above.

In the story we will examine today Jonah had to come to terms with these three: **sin, mercy, grace.**

BIBLE PASSAGE

Read Jonah 1:1-2:10 and use the space below to record any questions it brings to mind or things you notice.

The opening verses of the book of Jonah contain a difficult assignment for Jonah. What was he told to do?

What did Jonah do in response to God's instruction (Jonah 1:3)?

Lesson Twenty-One

Understand that God was preparing to throw a lifeline to the Assyrians, allowing them to repent from their evil and come into a relationship with Him. God's people were to be a blessing to all nations, and He wanted Jonah to be His instrument in this process.

Why do you think Jonah was so unwilling?

Interesting, isn't it? We have the ability, the prerogative, to say "no" to God. We have the freedom to choose to enter into what He is asking of us, or to refuse to be a part of it. Jonah refused to obey God's command, and went instead in the opposite direction.

Sin, simply put, is breaking God's law and rebelling against Him; choosing to do things our own way independent of God and His authority. Verse 3 says Jonah was "hoping to escape from the Lord." He wanted to shake free from God's authority over him, and sometimes we do too.

Later in Scripture, Jesus further clarified what sin is. He said the two most important things we must do are to love God and to love others. Whenever we run from this, choosing instead to love ourselves above all else, we are sinning.

With this definition of sin in mind, can you think of ways you have sinned? In what ways have you chosen to take things into your own hands and refuse God's authority?

Where have you loved yourself above God and others?

Verse 4 of Chapter 1 begins with these three words: "_____ _____ _____..."

Mercy! The Lord is about to interrupt Jonah's plans, showing mercy in an unexpected way.

What do you think Jonah deserved because of his blatant disobedience of God's expressed command?

Romans 6:23 sheds some light on this. What does it say is the punishment incurred by sin?

Verses 12-14 of Jonah 1 convey Jonah's understanding of what he deserves. What did he expect to happen to him?

What Jonah earned by his sin is the same as what we rightfully earn through our sin: death – separation from God. We have chosen to distance ourselves from God, so permanent separation from God would be the logical and deserved result of that.

However, God extends mercy to Jonah. Mercy is deliverance from judgement - God offering not to punishing us as our sins deserve.

In the same way God exercised mercy in His dealings with Jonah, He also was merciful with the sailors on the ship. Remember, these people were idol-worshipping pagan people. In verse 4 they had "shouted to their gods for help," but now the *true* God revealed Himself to them.

How did the sailors react to God's authority over the storm? (Jonah 1:16)

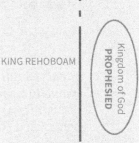

Verse 17 opens with these words: "Now the Lord had arranged…"

God *arranges* circumstances in order to demonstrate His mercy as He reaches out to people. Sometimes His mercy can look strange to us. (Mercy came in the form of a huge fish in Jonah's life.) But God persists with us, drawing us through circumstances and experiences, working to show us who He is, and reaching out to us to give us a second chance.

Can you think of ways God has reached out to you with His mercy?

Examine Jonah's prayer in chapter 2. Write below any phrases that you feel convey Jonah's response to the mercy God has shown him.

Grace is God extending His kindness to us, even though we do not deserve it. It is Him offering blessing in the face of our sin.

When studying the Bible, it is often helpful to look at the same verse in different translations. Read both of these versions of vs. 8:

> "Those who worship false gods turn their backs on all God's mercies." (NLT)

> "Those who cling to worthless idols forfeit the grace that could be theirs." (NIV)

How did we see the sailors on the boat experience the truths of verse 8?

Lesson Twenty-One

In what way does Jonah come to terms with these truths? What worthless idols had he clung to?

Read Chapters 3 and 4 of Jonah (it's only 22 verses) and you will see that Jonah still had a ways to go in grappling with God's grace.

In Jonah 3:5 and 10 what does it say ultimately happened when Jonah preached God's message to the Ninevites?

Hear what God's heart is toward these people, who were considered Israel's enemy, as it is expressed in Jonah 4:11. Sum it up here:

PRAYER MOMENT

Amazingly, no one is outside of God's mercy and grace. It is for everyone – the sailors, Jonah, the Ninevites…and it is for you. You simply need to be a sinner in order to qualify. It is not that God merely overlooks your sin and neglects to punish it, it is that He arranged for Jesus to be punished *in your place*. (See, I told you mercy can look strange!) Jesus' sacrifice on the cross satisfied the death you had earned through your sin. Hear this verse in it's entirely now: *"For the wages of sin is death, but the free gift of God is eternal life, through Christ Jesus our Lord." (Romans 6:23)* Have **you** responded to God's offer to give you eternal life instead of the eternal death your sin has earned you? Pray about this important question now as you close this lesson.

☐ *Check here when you have filled out your timeline with the new entries from this lesson.*

90   Finding Your Way

LESSON TWENTY-TWO

PRAYER MOMENT

God warns,

"If you do not serve the LORD your God with joy and enthusiasm for the abundant benefits you have received, you will serve your enemies whom the LORD will send against you."
(Deuteronomy 28:47-48a)

Pray for a heart to serve the Lord with **joy** and **enthusiasm** today.

BIBLE PASSAGE

Read II Kings 17:1-23 and use the space below to record any questions it brings to mind or things you notice.

A broken-down car, a burst pipe, an earthquake, a volcano. Some things in life *seem* sudden, but actually have been a long time in the making. Can you think of something you have experienced in life that was like this?

We arrive at a tragic turning point for the Northern Kingdom of Israel as we read II Kings 17. This chapter, which details the events which occurred in 722 B.C., literally documents the end of Israel's history. "How did they get to this point?" we ask as we read this chapter. It seems so sudden and severe, yet it had been a long time coming. The verse below contains a key to understanding the Lord's justice in this.

"And the people of Israel persisted in all the evil ways of Jeroboam.
They did not turn from these sins until the LORD finally swept them away from His presence,
just as all his prophets had warned." II Kings 17:23

Circle the phrases in the above verse which you think are the keys to understanding why God judged Israel at this point.

Scripture tells us about various prophets who were sent to Israel during the 200 years prior to this event. It was the prophet's job to serve as a voice crying out in the wilderness, to act as a light shining in the darkness. Do you remember what the crux of their message was? (Hint – it is summed up in the Hebrew word "shuv". Look back to lesson twenty if you don't remember.)

Kingdom of God Prophesied 91

Lesson Twenty-Two

II Kings 17:13 explains,

> "Again and again the LORD had sent his prophets and seers to warn both Israel and Judah:
>
> "_____ all your evil ways. _____ my commands and decrees…"

Before we study II Kings 17 further, let's backtrack and look at some of the prophets who were sent to Israel, so we can understand what they had been doing all these years. Fill in the column on the right, listing what the prophet is doing in the verses on the left. (I've started with the first one for you…)

NAME OF THE PROPHET	WHAT WE SEE THE PROPHET DOING
Elijah Prophesied from 853-798 BC *"Oh LORD, answer me! Answer me so these people will know that you, O LORD, are God and that you have brought them back to yourself."* *I Kings 18:37*	- *Praying for the people* - *Lifting God up before the people* - *Inviting people to return to God*
Micaiah Prophesied around 850 BC *The king's messenger said, "Look, (everyone) is promising victory for the king. Be sure that you agree with them and promise success." But Micaiah replied, "As surely as the LORD lives, I will say only what my God says."* *II Chronicles 18:12-13*	
AMOS Prophesied from 760-750 BC *"Listen to this message that the LORD has spoken against you, O people of Israel – Against the entire family I rescued from Egypt: "My people have forgotten how to do right," says the LORD. "Their fortresses are filled with wealth taken by theft and violence. Therefore," says the Sovereign LORD," an enemy is coming! He will surround them and shatter their defenses. Then he will plunder all their fortresses."* *Amos 3:1,10,11*	
Hosea Prophesied from 760-722 BC *"O people of Israel, do not rejoice as other nations do. For you have been unfaithful to your God, hiring yourselves out like prostitutes, worshiping other gods on every threshing floor. You may no longer stay here in the LORD's land. Instead, you will return to Egypt, and in Assyria you will eat food that is ceremonially unclean."* *Hosea 9:1,3*	

Now let's look back at II Kings 17. Verses 7 and 12 serve as bookends for the section that falls between them. Fill in the blanks in the two verses below:

Vs. 7: "This disaster came upon the people of Israel because they _____."

Vs. 12: "Yes, they _____, despite the LORD's specific and repeated warnings."

In the space above, between these two verses, add some details from verses 8-11 of how Israel had disobeyed.

Look also at verses 16-17 and add the details you find there to your list above.

These events may seem far removed from where you find yourself today, but can you find some similarities to your own life situation? In what ways does *our nation* reject God's authority, like the Israelites did?

In what ways do *your friends and family* reject the Lord's leadership over their lives?

PRAYER MOMENT

It is into this darkness that the Lord has called YOU to serve as a light, as the prophets did in their day. Look again at what you listed as the prophets' activities on the previous page. Spend some time in prayer asking God how you might serve your generation as the prophets once did. List here the things you think God is asking of you:

☐ *Check here when you have filled out your timeline with the new entries from this lesson.*

GOD

KING REHOBOAM — Kingdom of God PROPHESIED

KINGDOM SPLITS

North	South
Israel	Judah
19 Rulers	20 Rulers
None good	Some good
Shechem	Jerusalem
(Samaria)	

KING JEROBOAM | KING REHOBOAM

KING AHAB

ELIJAH

35. MICHAIAH

JONAH

36. AMOS

37. HOSEA

38. ASSYRIA ATTACKS AND CONQUERS

LESSON TWENTY-THREE

PRAYER MOMENT

Why do some people walk with God for a time, and then wander away? In prayer, ask God this question. Jot down any answers that come to mind below.

As we turn the page to today's lesson, **we are turning our attention to the Southern Kingdom of Judah**. We will be back-tracking chronologically, returning to the beginning of Judah's history, picking up shortly after the Northern Kingdom of Israel broke away from the Southern Kingdom.

BIBLE PASSAGE

Our text for today is II Chronicles 24:1-27. However, there is a significant "But" in the middle of this text, so you will be reading it in two segments. Begin by reading II Chronicles 24:1-16 and use the space below to record any questions it brings to mind or things you notice. (Remember: our focus has now turned to Judah, the Southern Kingdom.)

CAST OF CHARACTERS: Write a brief description of each of these as you encounter them in this narrative. (You can fill in the first two now, and the remaining three will come later in this lesson.)

JOASH:

JEHOIADA:

'LEADERS OF JUDAH':

PROPHETS

ZECHARIAH:

Summarize the story thus far.

How had the temple been destroyed (Vs. 7)?

What do you see that King Joash did well in this section?

How did the leaders and the people respond to Joash's building initiative (vs. 10)?

What is your impression of Jehoiada the priest?

Verse 2 specifies an important detail:

"Joash did what was pleasing in the LORD's sight throughout the lifetime of Jehoiada…"

Verse 14 hints at something similar:

"… and the burnt offerings were sacrificed continually in the Temple of the LORD during the lifetime of Jehoiada the priest."

What do you think is being foreshadowed in these verses? Circle the words in the verses above which hint at this.

Let's see how you did at predicting what was coming next in this story. Read II Chronicles 24:17-27. Fill in the rest of your cast of characters as you read.

Did you notice the significant "But" which opens this section? What event caused such a downturn in Joash's leadership? _____

To King Joash, Jehoiada was more than just a priest, he was actually a father figure. During Joash's childhood, his life was in danger because his grandmother was a wicked queen who wanted to wipe out all of the descendants of the previous king. "But the LORD did not want to destroy David's dynasty, for he had made a covenant with David and promised that his descendants would continue to rule, shining like a lamp forever." (II Chronicles 21:7) So, the Lord inspired Joash's aunt to protect him. This aunt was married to Jehoiada the priest and they together hid Joash in the temple and served as his foster parents.

Tragically, when the Priest Jehoiada died, King Joash no longer had this godly mentor who inspired Joash to lead the people toward God. He instead defaulted to heeding the prevailing voices of the "leaders," and he succumbed as they urged him to lead the people into idolatry.

Lesson Twenty-Three

Underline the verbs in this verse to see how this unfolded:

"…the leaders of Judah came and bowed before King Joash and persuaded him to listen to their advice. They decided to abandon the Temple of the LORD the God of their ancestors, and they worshiped Asherah poles and idols instead!"
II Chronicles 24:18

They came…they bowed…they persuaded…they decided…they worshipped. What are all the things that have gone wrong here?

This same story is also told in II Kings. Read II Kings 12:2-3. What had Joash unwisely allowed throughout his reign?

Why do you think the leaders wanted Judah to go back to idolatry?

Who did the LORD send to confront the people about their disobedience (II Chronicles 24:19-20)?

Look at how the leaders had vacillated over the years:

"This pleased the leaders…and they gladly brought their money (to repair the temple)" (Vs. 10)
"…the leaders…decided to abandon the Temple…and they worshiped Asherah poles and idols instead!" (Vs. 18)
"The leaders plotted to kill Zechariah (the priest) and King Joash ordered that they stone him to death in the courtyard of the LORD's temple." (Vs. 21)

Repair the temple…abandon the temple…murder God's priest in the temple. The leaders abandoned the truth and King Joash, no longer under the influence of his godly priest-mentor Jehoiada, joined them. It eventually led to his undoing. His reign came to a tragic end.

PRAYER MOMENT

Draw a match and a candle in the space in the margins.

Consider for a moment why one burns only briefly, and the other much longer. Label in your drawing above what causes this difference.
Joash was a match. Like the short-lived stick of a match, Joash had only a small fuel source that kept him burning bright: his priest Jehoiada. When Jehoiada was gone, Joash burned out.

Which are you – a long-burning candle or a short-lived match? What fuels your faith and your desire to obey the Lord? Are you dependent only on one person, as Joash was? Or do you have a number of factors which energize your walk with the Lord. Are there things you should <u>add</u> into your life which would help fuel you and keep you from burning out? Spend some time thinking about these questions and journal a brief prayer below.

☐ *Check here when you have filled out your timeline with the new entries from this lesson.*

Finding Your Way

LESSON TWENTY-FOUR

PRAYER MOMENT

"…God has made everything beautiful for its own time. He has planted eternity in the human heart, but even so, people cannot see the whole scope of God's work from beginning to end."
Ecclesiastes 3:11

Pray that today God will show you what it means that He has "planted eternity in your heart."

Before we move on, let's review what we have learned. See if you can complete this chart:

LOCATION	NAME OF KINGDOM	# OF RULERS	ANY GOOD RULERS?	CAPITAL CITY		
North	I			S ( )		
South	J			J		

*We'll fill in these new columns later

Yesterday we examined the life of King Joash, which was a mixed bag. How would you describe him?

Unfortunately, Joash is a fairly typical representation of the kings in general. We say in our chart above that in the South there were "some good kings." However, only a few were stellar at following the Lord in faith and obedience throughout their entire lives.

Two additional pieces of information will round out our chart above. The first empty column should be entitled "Family Line." Have you picked up on what family line continues throughout the history of the Southern Kingdom? If not, it will help if we reflect on where this all began.

You will recall that the first Israelite king was Saul, who was a false start for God's people. They had insisted on a king at the wrong time and with the wrong motivation, and ended up with a king who was all wrong for them.

The second king, however, was God's anointed man: King David, a "man after God's own heart." Although not perfect, he led the people well, and his son Solomon then followed him. Solomon led with wisdom in many ways but made the fatal mistake of enslaving his own people to complete his lavish building projects.

Solomon escaped the consequence of his wrongdoing during his lifetime, but his son, Rehoboam, reaped the penalty of his father's choices. It was at this point that Jeroboam incited the people to revolt, which split the Northern Kingdom (called "Israel") from the Southern one (named "Judah").

Lesson Twenty-Four

Amazingly, the Southern Kingdom continues with David's family line throughout its entire history. The twenty kings who came and went over the 350 years of Judah's history are all a part of David's lineage. Not so in the Northern Kingdom. Theirs is a much more tumultuous history. Over the Northern Kingdom's history of only 200 years nineteen kings reigned from nine different families. Every change of family line in Israel was accomplished through upheaval. On your chart on the previous page label the last column "Duration," and fill in the total number of years the kingdoms of Israel and Judah lasted, as explained here.

We must marvel at how the Lord preserved His work in the Southern Kingdom…all leading up to its culmination, which is yet to come in our study. Today's reading will give us a hint as to where this is all going.

BIBLE PASSAGE

Read Isaiah 11:1-16 and use the space below to record any questions it brings to mind or things you notice.

What is described here sounds idyllic. Surely this leader is vividly different from any King we have documented thus far in our study. God's rule and blessing are seen here in ways we have never seen before!

Verse 1 begins with a "new shoot" from an "old root."
Use this space to draw what is described here, and label the parts as they are explained in that verse.

Somehow David's family tree has been previously chopped down, but this Scripture provides hope. What do you think this verse is alluding to?

A description of this "new shoot" is provided in verses 1-5. Complete the phrase "He will…" by listing what is explained about him in these verses. Put a star next to the qualities which you feel are especially important in a leader.

He will…

This is painting a picture of a powerful King who rules with wisdom, insight, and justice, empowered by the Spirit of God…just what the people had longed for during the nearly 500 years they had been led by a king. Remember, back in I Samuel 8, how they had insisted "We want a king just like all the other nations." Well, that is exactly what they received. King after king who was no better than the kings of other nations – human, flawed, disappointing. But the leader who is described here in Isaiah 11 is something entirely different. *This* is what the people had been longing for.

Let's continue to verses 6-16 to see how far reaching the impact of this king is. Complete the phrase "In that day…" listing what will go on under this king's rule.

In that day…

The impact of this leader falls into two categories: **Peace Among Creation** and **Peace Among God's People**. Label each of these categories on your "In that day..."list on the previous page.

Don't miss this first one: peace among creation. The impact of this King will extend even into the natural world. The peace which he brings affects predators and prey so they exist in harmony together? Amazing! Think of the most recent presidential election when you listened to the extensive campaign promises of each candidate. Sure, they made some impressive promises, but none of them claimed to be able to accomplish this kind of change in the world's natural order.

Do you wonder who this king would be? Read verse 10 again:

> *"In that day the heir to David's throne will be a banner of salvation to all the world.*
> *The nations will rally to him, and the land where he lives will be a glorious place."*

The key to unlocking this chapter is to know who this "banner of salvation" is. The kings up until this point had done little to save the people. Yes, God's people experienced various victories along the way, but it never lasted. And here Judah was, dreading the captivity that this prophet Isaiah continually warned was coming for them, as it had come to Israel in the north. All of God's people: captive. Who could save them permanently, eternally? It would surely need to be a king much greater than those Israel had ever known. The king to whom this prophecy is pointing is **Jesus**!

Flip a few pages back in your Bible and read Isaiah 9:6-7. This familiar passage we immediately recognize as referring to Jesus because we often hear it read at Christmastime.

What truths about Jesus are explained here which were also found in our reading today?

Take some time and ponder what the people of Judah were yearning for at this moment in their history. What do you think they longed for deep down?

PRAYER MOMENT

We are always longing for more than this world can supply. We yearn to go back to the way creation was at the beginning – whole, beautiful, unbroken. Spend some time in prayer considering what you are longing for today which is beyond what this world can provide.

The answer to this longing is today as it was in Isaiah's time. The answer to your yearning is **Jesus**. He is the healer, the restorer, the one who brings freedom and harmony. We can experience a glimpse of this in our lives, as Jesus begins to heal our brokenness. However, the ultimate healing and restoration comes for us in eternity with Jesus.

> *"Nothing will hurt or destroy in all my holy mountain,*
> *for as the waters fill the sea, so the earth will be filled with people who know the LORD.*
> *In that day the heir to David's throne will be a banner of salvation to all the world*
> *...and the land where He lives will be a glorious place." Isaiah 11:9-10*

That, my friend, is what I am longing for... It is what you are longing for.

LESSON TWENTY-FIVE

> ## PRAYER MOMENT
>
> *"The LORD, the God of their ancestors, repeatedly sent His prophets to warn them, for He had compassion on His people and His temple. But the people mocked these messengers of God and despised their words. They scoffed at the prophets until the LORD's anger could no longer be restrained and nothing could be done." II Chronicles 36:15-16*
>
> In prayer, reflect on the compassion and patience you have seen the Lord exercise toward His people thus far in the unfolding story of the Bible.

There I was in the hardware store, standing in line and watching the mother in front of me being worked over by her preschooler. This was one disobedient little rascal! The child simply refused to resist the urge to climb on a riding lawn mower on display at the front of the store. Up he went. "Timmy don't climb on that," corrected his mother. "I'm just joking Mommy," he replied in his innocent four year old voice. Then back up he went. Again, "Timmy, don't climb on that." To which he responded, "I'm just joking, Mommy." Admittedly, he was a cute kid, but something within me cried out for the child to experience a consequence for his persistent disobedience. Who was in charge here after all?

Can you relate? Maybe you remember a time when you witnessed continual disobedience, and knew a consequence was in order.

It is with this sense that we open to our passage today. God has persisted and patiently persevered with His people in the Southern Kingdom of Judah for 350 years. They have failed to obey Him time after time, hurtling into idolatry and conformity. Rather than worshipping God and embracing the uniqueness of their relationship with the Creator, they abandoned Him. Keep this backdrop in mind as you open to today's reading.

> ## BIBLE PASSAGE
>
> Read Jeremiah 52:1-30 and use the space below to record any questions it brings to mind or things you notice.

What you just read was written by the prophet Jeremiah, a prophet who had an exhausting call on his life. Assigned with the job of prophesying to the people of Judah during the final 40 years of their history, he faithfully warned the people. But his words were utterly disregarded by them. He is known as "the Weeping Prophet" because he mourned as he stood by and watched the people refuse God's offer of repentance and restoration. He knew full well what this meant for them: destruction. Today's reading, you will notice, is the last chapter of the book of Jeremiah which details what took place after all of Jeremiah's prophesying.

Read Jeremiah 52:1-3. Who was the king at this point in Judah's history? _____

What kind of king was King Zedekiah? Good or Evil (circle one)
"Why another evil king?" we ask. The answer is found in verse 3… what is the reason?

A passage in II Kings parallels this one, so we need to read II Kings 24:2-4 to understand what had taken Judah to this tipping point. What information does this section add?

Wonder who this King Manasseh is? Read II Kings 21:1-9 to get a glimpse of just how evil this King of Judah was. List the evil things this king did:

Now return to our reading in Jeremiah 52. Verses 4-11 sound like the plot of a Hollywood movie! List the main events here:

Verses 4-11 highlight what happened to the king. Verses 12-27 give details about what was going on, meanwhile, back in the city…

What happens to the city and walls?

What happens to the people?

What happens to the temple?

What happens to the city leaders?

Complete the following, using verses 28-30:

King Nebuchadnezzar attacks and takes people of Judah to _____ in three waves.

Reading this, it may be hard to grasp what this felt like to God's people. But imagine what this would look like if something comparable happened to our country: significant landmarks and fortifications destroyed, churches targeted and demolished, leaders of our nation taken away and brutally executed, leading citizens taken captive and carried away to a foreign land. Only the poorest of the poor allowed to stay, eking a life out of the rubble which remained.

GOD

KING REHOBOAM — Kingdom of God PROPHESIED

KINGDOM SPLITS

North	South
Israel	Judah
19 Rulers	20 Rulers
None good	Some good
Shechem (Samaria)	Jerusalem

KING JEROBOAM — KING REHOBOAM

KING AHAB

ELIJAH

MICHAIAH

KING JOASH
PRIEST JEHOIDA

JONAH

AMOS

HOSEA

ASSYRIA ATTACKS AND CONQUERS

41. KING ZEDEKIAH

BABYLON ATTACKS AND CONQUERS

This is a point in the history of God's people which manifests God's **justice**. Reflect on who the Lord revealed Himself to be, when He met with Moses on Mt. Sinai:

"Then the LORD came down in a cloud and stood there with him; and He called out His own name, Yahweh. The LORD passed in front of Moses, calling out, "Yahweh! The LORD!" The God of compassion and mercy! I am slow to anger and filled with unfailing love and faithfulness. I lavish unfailing love to a thousand generations. I forgive iniquity, rebellion, and sin. But I do not excuse the guilty. I lay the sins of the parents upon their children and grandchildren; the entire family is affected — even children in the third and fourth generations."
Exodus 34:5-7

Which of the Lord's qualities listed in these verses were manifest at this point in history when Jerusalem was destroyed? Circle those qualities.

Now remember the story of Jonah, which we covered in lesson 23. Underline in the verses above the qualities of God which were evident in that story.

The character of God is a unified whole. He is both compassionate and righteous, gracious and holy, forgiving and just. His response to man exhibits His whole character, in the right way at the right time. We can rest in the fact that He does this perfectly. There comes a time when sin is persistent and unrepentant that it is right for Him to enact consequences. And that is what He did here in Jeremiah 52. It was right for the people to be punished and carried off into captivity.

PRAYER MOMENT

When our hearts cry out for justice in this world, we are actually reflecting something of the image of God. We need to rest in the fact that God sees, God knows, God cares. God will be just when He acts at the perfect time. Take a few minutes now to pray about any areas in which you yearn to see God's justice enacted. You can list these areas below:

☐ *Check here when you have filled out your timeline with the new entries from this lesson.*

LESSON TWENTY-SIX

PRAYER MOMENT

Personalize these words into a prayer as you begin your study today:

"We wait in hope for the Lord: He is our help and our shield."
Psalm 33:20

A graveyard…inherently one of the most hopeless places on earth. That is where our study begins today. At a bleak point in the history of God's people, while they are languishing as exiles in Babylon, God takes His prophet Ezekiel to a desolate valley to paint for him a hopeful picture of what is ahead for Judah.

BIBLE PASSAGE

Read Ezekiel 37:1-14 and use the space below to record any questions it brings to mind or things you notice.

As you read verses 1 and 2, what do you notice about these bones?

How do you think all these bones came to be like this?

Then, in verse 3, comes the question: "Can these bones become living people again?"

What is the common-sense answer to this?   What is the faith-driven answer Ezekiel provided?

We know how things *usually* work… but we can't know how they will work *when the Lord is involved*. We do not know His plan, His resources, and His power which He will exercise in the situation at hand.

Kingdom of God Prophesied 103

Lesson Twenty-Six

Don't miss how Ezekiel addressed the Lord in verse 3. What name did he use for God?

Think that through. What do each of those words mean? Write a paraphrase next to it above.

In verse 4 Ezekiel is instructed to "speak a prophetic message to these bones." Our instinctive response is "How on earth can that help?" What we know of words doesn't lead us to believe that this would have any impact. But consider what we know about GOD's words from Hebrews 4:12:

"For the Word of God is alive and active. It is sharper than the sharpest two-edged sword, cutting between soul and spirit, between joint and marrow. It exposes our innermost thoughts and desires."

God's word is in an entirely different category and is active in a supernatural way. This is a game-changer. Ezekiel was then instructed to convey three God-dictated prophesies to these dried up and scattered bones, and each prophecy accomplished its intended impact.

PROPHECY #1: (Vs. 4-6)	**RESULT:** (Vs. 7-8)
"Dry bones, listen to the word of the LORD! This is what the Sovereign LORD says: Look! I am going to put breath into you and make you live again! I will put flesh and muscles on you and cover you with skin. I will put breath into you and you will come to life. Then you will know that I am the LORD."	

In the verses above there is a clear emphasis on the Lord and His activity. Circle all of the references to God. List the results of this prophecy in the column on the right.

Ezekiel spoke and there were immediate results! Scattered bones came together, attached themselves as complete skeletons – from the bulky femur to the minuscule, delicate anvil bone – all parts in place. Muscle and flesh and skin formed. Where did that come from? Out of thin air! The Lord doesn't need any material to work with. He can create out of nothing.

PROPHECY #2: (Vs. 9)	**RESULT:** (Vs. 10)
"This is what the Sovereign LORD says: Come, O breath, from the four winds. Breathe into these dead bodies so they may live again."	

Again, circle the reference to God's name here. Then list the results.

Certain prophecies, when they are given, provide no precise interpretation within the text. We are left to infer what they relate to. However, we are not left wondering here in Ezekiel 37. The interpretation is given by the Lord Himself in verse 11.

What do these hopeless, dried up, scattered, lifeless, defeated old bones represent?

Ezekiel is then commissioned to speak out this explanation to the great, resurrected army of bones.

PROPHECY #3: (Vs. 12-14)

"This is what the Sovereign LORD says: O my people, I will open your graves of exile and cause you to rise again. Then I will bring you back to the land of Israel. When this happens, O my people, you will know that I am the LORD. I will put my Spirit in you, and you will live again and return home to your own land. Then you will know that I, the LORD, have spoken and I have done what I said. Yes, the LORD has spoken!"

RESULT:

Once again, circle all the references to God's name here. We don't see immediate results here, but what does the prophecy detail, which we should be on the lookout for in our upcoming days of study? List under "results."

So, although our initial response was that words have no power to bring dead bones back to life, we see that

"With man this is impossible, but not with God; all things are possible with God."
(Mark 10:27, NIV)

This chapter opened with a scene that appeared to be utter defeat – bones scattered across the valley after a great battle which had been lost. However, what does verse 10 say about these bones at the end of this miracle? They are "a great _____." These lifeless bones have been fully restored and are ready to engage again - strengthened to overcome in the next battle they would face. This was what was ahead for the kingdom of Judah.

PRAYER MOMENT

How can this give us hope today? Reflect for a moment on your own life. Where do you feel all dried up, lifeless, and perhaps scattered? Do you find yourself out of patience, low on energy, without joy, and lacking resources for what you are facing? Maybe you have nothing left for the needs facing you, and you feel defeated. Spend a moment considering how this relates to you today.

As you face the question, "Can my hopeless situation come to life again?", you must remember that the answer is only found in our Sovereign Lord. He alone can resurrect what is dead. God's word has the power to create, to bring life where there is none. *He* is the **Sovereign Lord**. Know that the answer to your need is rooted in who God is, not in what you bring to the process. Realize that if you are a follower of Jesus, He has already done the most important resurrection work in your life, bringing you from death to life. You can trust Him with what concerns you today, so commit the needs you contemplated above to the Lord in prayer now.

☐ *Check here when you have filled out your timeline with the new entries from this lesson.*

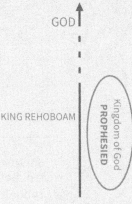

GOD ↑

KING REHOBOAM — Kingdom of God PROPHESIED

KINGDOM SPLITS

North	South
Israel	Judah
19 Rulers	20 Rulers
None good	Some good
Shechem	Jerusalem
(Samaria)	

KING JEROBOAM | KING REHOBOAM

KING AHAB

ELIJAH

MICHAIAH

KING JOASH
PRIEST JEHOIDA

JONAH

AMOS

HOSEA

ASSYRIA ATTACKS AND CONQUERS

BABYLON ATTACKS AND CARRIES SOME AWAY, INCLUDING
42. EZEKIEL

KING ZEDEKIAH

BABYLON ATTACKS AND CONQUERS

↓

LESSON TWENTY-SEVEN

PRAYER MOMENT

If you are familiar with some of the stories of the Bible, this will probably be one you have heard before. As you read, remember that this is an actual historical account, not a storybook fable. Look at this story with fresh eyes today, asking the Lord what you personally can learn from this story.

"All Scripture is inspired by God and is useful to teach us what is true and to make us realize what is wrong in our lives. It corrects us when we are wrong and teaches us to do what is right. God uses it to prepare and equip His people to do every good work."
II Timothy 3:16-17

"How can we sing the Lord's song in a foreign land?" lamented the people of Judah during their exile in Babylon. (Psalm 137:4) It was a pressing question. How were they to maintain their faith and their distinctiveness while immersed in the pagan culture of Babylon? They hadn't successfully maintained their holiness when they were in their own land, and now they were surrounded by opposition on all sides.

Actually, it is not that different from the dilemma we face in our nation today. How do *we* sing the Lord's song in *our* land? Faced, as we are, with a culture which has swept every trace of the Lord's presence from its public life, a culture which lives for pleasure, how do we successfully live for and speak for God? We have much to learn from Daniel today.

Chosen because he was one of the cream-of-the-crop, Daniel was carried off to Babylon when he was a young man. There he lived out his life with consistent faith and integrity, weathering the reigns of multiple kings in two successive empires. Daniel was one of the top administrators under each ruler. However, it wasn't always an easy task.

BIBLE PASSAGE

Read Daniel 6:1-28 and use the space below to record any questions it brings to mind or things you notice.

From Daniel 6:3-4, list all of the descriptive terms given for Daniel.

Daniel excelled beyond his peers as he faithfully exercised his God-given gifts of leadership. This attracted the attention of the king…and the jealousy of his peers.

When Daniel edged them out for an important promotion, they looked for a way to take him down. They found only one. What was it (Vs. 5)?

Could that be said of you? Do you live a life which is so holy, so above reproach, that you could be criticized only because of your faith? Or would those you live and work with find other things to accuse you about first?

Not only did the other administrators know Daniel's true colors, they also knew their king's true colors. King Darius was an arrogant leader, so they played to his ego while simultaneously setting a trap for Daniel.

What did they say to the king to stroke his ego (Vs. 6-8)?

The insincerity of their plan is thinly veiled. If you look closely, you'll see that they didn't want to permanently sell-out to worshipping the king. No, they set limits on this law, so they could go back to doing whatever they wanted after 30 days. Just long enough to trap Daniel, they figured.

Little did the king know that this law, so casually signed, would bring him to a point of crisis. First, however, Daniel would be faced with a crisis of his own when he learned about the law.

Daniel's Response to Crisis (Read Vs. 10-11)

What crisis did Daniel face?

List what Daniel did in response to this crisis (be specific):

Look between the words here and see if you can find what Daniel's demeanor was. How would you describe his emotion?

As you read this account, what do you imagine his prayer might have been?

Dear Lord…

Amen.

He prayed "as usual." Three times a day "as always." What do these phrases tell us about Daniel?

It is no surprise what we find Daniel doing when the officials barge into his house. What was Daniel doing in verse 11?

This chapter of Scripture gives us a clear contrast by placing **Daniel** and **King Darius** side-by-side. They are both faced with a crisis and react in entirely different ways. Now let's look at King Darius to see what his response to calamity looked like.

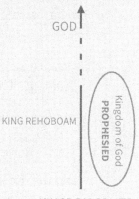

107

Lesson Twenty-Seven

Have you ever tried to solve a problem and found that you instead made a much bigger problem? That is what Darius now had to grapple with.

What problem had King Darius created when he signed this law (Vs. 13-14)?

Darius' Response to Crisis (Read Vs. 14-20)

What crisis did King Darius face?

List all of the things King Darius did in response to this crisis (be specific):

If we are not fully dependent on and anchored to God and His resources, the only response we can have to crisis is panic. We must grab the reigns and scramble to control the situation.

Reflecting on the two characters we have studied today, how do you tend to respond to crisis?

How had Daniel survived this ordeal? He did what he had been doing all along – in the easy times before the law was passed, under pressure after the law had been passed, and now in the crisis of the lions' den. Verse 23:

"he _____ his _____."

A few years ago, I watched as Lynne, a young wife and mother at my church, struggled through a tragic decline due to cancer. I learned that there were times when her pain was so great that she could not even open her eyes. She was alone in her thoughts; yet not alone, because all the Scripture she had memorized over her lifetime came flooding in, bringing comfort to her in this place of despair. Before she went home to heaven, she told me something I'll never forget. **"When the crisis hits, there is no time to build a spiritual foundation."** Lynne was prepared. She had made decisions in the good times to prepare for the hard times.

Daniel had, too. When faced with the lions he prayed "as always" and "as usual." He was ready.

PRAYER MOMENT

Interestingly, King Darius ends in this chapter in the same place where Daniel began: praising and honoring the Lord. Read aloud, if possible, the words Darius spoke in verses 26-27. King Darius' words provide a good pattern for praising God. Pray these phrases for yourself.

He is _____
_{What is something you know about God's character?}

He will _____
_{What is something you know He has promised?}

His kingdom will _____
_{What do you know about God's kingdom?}

His rule will _____
_{How will God rule?}

He rescues _____
_{Who does God rescue?}

He performs _____
_{What have you seen God do?}

He has rescued _____
_{In what way has God rescued you?}

☐ *Check here when you have filled out your timeline with the new entries from this lesson.*

108 Finding Your Way

LESSON TWENTY-EIGHT

PRAYER MOMENT

Is God sovereign over the political events of our world? As you consider that question, ask the Lord to help you discover this today.

> *"Praise the name of God forever and ever, for He has all wisdom and power. He controls the course of world events; He removes kings and sets up other kings."*
> Daniel 2:20-21

Remember in yesterday's lesson you learned that Daniel lived during the administration of multiple kings under <u>two different empires</u>? King Darius, who we studied yesterday, overthrew the empire of Babylon, ushering in the Medo-Persian empire. As the Persian empire progressed, King Cyrus came to the throne in 538 BC and miraculously, God moved in his heart in a way that favored the Jews.

BIBLE PASSAGE

Read Ezra 3:1-13 and use the space below to record any questions it brings to mind or things you notice.

Curious about what had gone on in the months before this rebuilding project began? Read Ezra 1:1-7.

What did God prompt this pagan king to instruct his people to do?

How had God prepared the Jews?

This event had been prophesied by Jeremiah in 605 BC, and the prophecy unfolded in history with remarkable accuracy. Underline anything you find interesting in the following verse:

> *"This entire land will become a desolate wasteland. Israel and her neighboring lands will serve the king of Babylon for seventy years. Then, after the seventy years of captivity are over, I will punish the king of Babylon and his people for their sins," says the LORD.*
> Jeremiah 25:12

Imagine it: the people had been told ahead of time that their captivity in Babylon would last seventy years. Do you think they had been watching the calendar, waiting for the years to pass, yearning to go home? Or had they lost hope of ever returning to their homeland, instead making the best of their lives in Babylon?

It seems that both things occurred. When offered the opportunity to return, about 50,000 Jews traveled back to their homeland. However many remained in Babylon.

Lesson Twenty-Eight

Why do you think some left and some stayed?

As Ezra 3 opens, we see that the Israelites assembled in Jerusalem with a "unified purpose" (vs. 1-2). What was it?

REBUILDING THE _____

What did this represent to them?

Ezra 3:3 specifies, "Even though the people were _____ of the local residents, they rebuilt the altar..." What might they have feared?

Before they laid the foundation for the temple, they did a number of things in obedience and worship in vs. 4-5. (Summarize what they did by looking for the <u>verbs</u> in these verses.)

They...

They had been given a second chance at living life in God's presence. What a great place for them to begin!

We also have been given the opportunity to live life in God's presence. What a great place for us to begin as we walk out our faith each day. Consider what this could look like for you:

- To <u>celebrate</u> your history with God.
- To honor Him by <u>living sacrificially</u>.
- To <u>offer</u> to Him things which are precious to you.
- To <u>give voluntarily</u> to the Lord.

Now the Israelites moved on to the second portion of their project. What was it? (Ezra 3:8)

REBUILDING THE _____

What had they done to prepare for this part of the rebuilding? (vs. 7)

Who made up the workforce? (vs. 8)

Upon completion of the foundation in verse 10, they took their places and praised the Lord, just as _____ had prescribed.

Earlier, we read in Vs. 2 that they sacrificed as instructed in the law of _____.

110 Finding Your Way

What did these two leaders represent to them?

Write below the words of praise they sang at this celebration (Vs. 11):

From what you know of the Israelite's experiences, paraphrase what you think they may have been saying in their hearts through these words of praise:

Read verses 12-13. Suddenly there is a somber note in the midst of this celebratory moment in Biblical history. Who was weeping?

What might they have been thinking?

Rebuilding all that had been lost was an overwhelming prospect. But they had been given a chance to be restored and they were determined not to waste it. Isn't the Lord good?! Sometimes we, like the Jews, blatantly disregard His call on our lives, and sell out to sin and disobedience. At other times, we simply wander off, busy and distracted with life, preoccupied with the agenda of the world all around us. But He continually gives us the opportunity to return to Him and to make Him top priority in our lives once again.

Where do you find yourself today? Ask yourself: "When I am invited to follow the Lord wholeheartedly once again, am I **determined not to waste this opportunity to be restored**?"

> The Jews began with worship and obedience…do I?
>
> The Jews learned through their pain and difficulty…have I?
>
> The Jews learned through others' experiences…have I?
>
> The Jews listened to the prophets…do I listen to the truth-tellers who speak into my life?
>
> The Jews listened to Moses' law…do I listen to Scripture?

(Spend a moment pondering the questions above. Note the areas you are doing well, and the ones which need more attention in your life.)

PRAYER MOMENT

Now spend a moment in prayer about what you have learned through this passage.

☐ *Check here when you have filled out your timeline with the new entries from this lesson.*

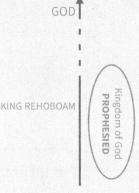

GOD

KING REHOBOAM — Kingdom of God PROPHESIED

KINGDOM SPLITS

North	South
Israel	Judah
19 Rulers	20 Rulers
None good	Some good
Shechem	Jerusalem
(Samaria)	

KING JEROBOAM | KING REHOBOAM

KING AHAB

ELIJAH

MICHAIAH

KING JOASH
PRIEST JEHOIDA

JONAH

AMOS

HOSEA

ASSYRIA ATTACKS AND CONQUERS

BABYLON ATTACKS AND CARRIES SOME AWAY, INCLUDING DANIEL

BABYLON ATTACKS AND CARRIES SOME AWAY, INCLUDING EZEKIEL

KING ZEDEKIAH

BABYLON ATTACKS AND CONQUERS

44. KING CYRUS

45. REBUILT ALTAR & TEMPLE

BONUS LESSON

> ## PRAYER MOMENT
>
> Is there an area of your life where you feel God is being silent right now? Spend some time talking to Him about that as you begin your study today.

Have you ever planned a surprise party? Remember the numerous details you had to orchestrate to make it all come off without a hitch? Invitations, food, activities. And most importantly, how would you get the guest of honor to the party unaware? All of this was done behind the scenes in secrecy and silence, and your heart was racing up until the perfect moment when everyone yelled "Surprise!"

What appeared to be a time of silence was actually a time of great activity. You were getting all the pieces in place for that perfect moment when everything would be unveiled.

In this Bonus Lesson we are going to look at the "**400 Years of Silence**" between the Old and New Testaments. This **Intertestamental Period** was a period of *silence*, in that there were no prophets speaking during these 400 years and there is no record of this time period in the Bible. But that does not mean it was a time of *inactivity* on God's part. He was diligently at work, readying the world for the appearance of His Son. And He would orchestrate this perfectly!

Since no Scripture was written during this time period, we have no Bible Passage for this lesson.

Before examining the Intertestamental Period, let's reflect on where we were as the Old Testament closed.

What has been the same between God and man since the beginning of time?

In what ways was God present with man in the Old Testament?

Where are the Jews found at the end of the Old Testament?

What is the whole Old Testament preparing for?

Now let's take a look at what God put in place during the 400 years between the Old and New Testaments, leading up to the moment when the Messiah would come on the scene.

GREEK LANGUAGE
Alexander the Great was a powerful leader who left a long-standing mark on the people during his reign from 356 – 323 B.C. Committed to standardizing and unifying the culture as a whole, Alexander required all of the people whom he had conquered in the Mediterranean world to speak the same language: Greek.

How do you imagine this would be strategically used by God when Jesus came to earth?

SYNAGOGUES
During the 400 years between the Testaments the Jews had been dispersed into far flung regions. In an effort to maintain their traditions, history, and distinctiveness, they set up synagogues in the towns where they settled. These were safe places for the Jews to gather and to remember who they were and where they had come from. Places to gather and to read Scripture together.

How do you think these synagogues would eventually be used to spread the news of Jesus?

PEACE
When Rome conquered the Mediterranean world, a period of peace known as the Pax Romana (the "Peace of Rome") ensued. This was a time of safety for the people in which they could thrive. Freedom of religion was tolerated by Rome during this window of time.

In what ways would this peace pave the way for people to come to hear about Jesus?

ROADS
During this time of peace, trade routes became well established throughout the region, with Jerusalem at the center of the hub. Paved roads allowed people to come and go easily, and with the people came their news and ideas.

How would these roads facilitate the spread of the Good News about Jesus?

In the space in the margin above draw an icon to remember each of these important factors: Greek Language, Synagogues, Peace, and Roads.

GOD

INTERTESTAMENTAL PERIOD
400 YEARS
GREEK LANGUAGE
SYNAGOGUES
PEACE
ROADS

Bonus Lesson

Galatians 4:4 (NASB) says, "But **when the fullness of time came**, God sent forth His Son…" In what ways was it the "fullness of time" when Jesus was born?

PRAYER MOMENT

Dear Lord,

Help me to remember that You are always at work, even during what appears to be a period of silence.

I today, choose to trust that You are at work in the following areas:

_____

_____

_____

_____

Lord, I pray You are putting things in place perfectly – preparing for what is **Your best** which is yet to come. I praise You for Your ability to do all things perfectly!

In Jesus Name,
Amen

☐ *Check here when you have filled out your timeline with the new entries from this lesson.*

LESSON TWENTY-NINE

> ## PRAYER MOMENT
>
> *"When you call on me, when you come and pray to me, I'll listen."*
> Jeremiah 29:12
>
> As you open your study today, pray that you'll trust God to hear and answer your prayers.

Do you recall where we left off in our Kingdom of God theme? (Look back on your timeline to be reminded.)

KINGDOM OF GOD _____

Remember that the activity of the prophets marked this long period of time during which: the kings ruled, the kingdom divided, both the north and south were conquered by foreign nations, and then Judah was permitted to return to the land.

What messages did these prophets bring to the people?

Beyond speaking into the issues of the day, these prophets pointed far ahead to the day when the Lord God would literally come down to earth. This is the culmination of all they spoke about. A Deliverer was coming who would be the Messiah. God would not leave the people in the dark, however. They were to remain alert for a sign, which would precede the Messiah, signifying that He was about to come. The prophet Malachi closes the Old Testament telling the people of this sign:

> *"Look! I am sending my messenger, and he will prepare the way before me.*
> *Then the Lord you are seeking will suddenly come to His Temple. The messenger of the covenant,*
> *whom you look for so eagerly, is surely coming," says the LORD of Heaven's Armies."*
> Malachi 3:1

> *"Look, I am sending you the prophet Elijah before the great and dreadful day of the the LORD arrives.*
> *His preaching will turn the hearts of fathers to their children, and the hearts of children to their fathers…"*
> Malachi 4:5-6

Underline above the words used to describe this person who would come before the Messiah.

They were told to look and to wait…and then 400 years of silence ensued…What were they to think?

When have you recently had to wait excessively for something and struggled to remain patient?

Sometimes during times of waiting we are tempted to give up. We determine it's not worth it, or maybe it's just never going to happen. The priest Zechariah found himself disillusioned from waiting and looking as the book of Luke opens.

Lesson Twenty-Nine

BIBLE PASSAGE

Read Luke 1:5-25 and use the space below to record any questions it brings to mind or things you notice.

List below the phrases used to describe Zechariah and Elizabeth in verses 5-7:

ZECHARIAH: **ELIZABETH:**

How was Zechariah chosen in verses 8-10 to enter the Temple that day? _____

This was perhaps a once in a lifetime experience, and God was in control of this random drawing of lots to get *this* man into the temple on *this* day so that he could receive *this* important message.

The angel opens with these words in verse 13, "Don't be afraid, Zechariah! God has heard your prayer." What prayer? From the context, what prayer do you think Zechariah and Elizabeth prayed?

From verses 13-17, list all the details about this child the angel is promising to Zechariah:

Now reflect back on Malachi's prophesies, which you read earlier in today's lesson. What words or phrases overlap with the message the angel gave to Zechariah?

Paraphrase what Zechariah is saying in his response in verse 18.

In verses 19-20, how does the angel handle Zechariah's poor response?

116 Finding Your Way

Imagine how this scene played out:

There he stands, in the dark solemnity of the temple's holy place. Offering prayers for his people, and remembering a lifetime of his own prayers. A stab of deep disappointment pierces Zechariah as he recalls the many years he and Elizabeth had prayed…for a child. Those prayers had gone unanswered.

Lost in the emotion of those memories, Zechariah is jolted awake by the blazing presence of an angel before him in this silent place. Zechariah is shaken and overwhelmed with fear. The words of the angel rattle him further – down to the core of his most painful disappointments with the God whom he serves.

He guards himself with thoughts of doubt. "I refuse to believe this promise," he thinks, "This is impossible, it's just too late." And words tumble from his unguarded lips "How can I be sure this will happen? I am an old man and my wife is also well along in years." He would protect himself from further disappointment by being really sure – he needed a good explanation. But what he was voicing simply boiled down to a lack of trust in his God. And even doubt in his God's wisdom. "Why would this make sense now?!" Ironically, those words of doubt would be the last he would utter until the promise was fulfilled.

God's timing often involves a lot of waiting.
- 400 years between the Old and New Testaments
- Decades between Zechariah and Elizabeth's prayers and this answer

…all to get to God's perfect moment…for the pieces of the puzzle to be used in the way He has in mind…in His perfect way and for His glory.
God is not afraid of the waiting period like we are. He is not going anywhere – He literally has all the time in the world.

Why are we afraid of waiting?

But the waiting can be a gift. It is a time of suspense, when you depend on the Lord, and constantly lay all your hopes and fears before Him. *This is communion with God* – sharing all of your deepest yearnings and listening for His voice. We don't depend on Him well in the easy times. Enough of your life must be out of your control so you to come to Him, in brokenness and neediness, and cast yourself at His feet.

What had Zechariah and Elizabeth asked God for? How had God's answer been beyond what they had asked for? (See Luke 1:57-66.)

PRAYER MOMENT

The answer to the prayer of these two godly people was greater than they would have ever asked for! **When the answer to your prayer involves a long wait, it may be because God is up to something so BIG that it requires time to put it all together!** Zechariah got it in the end. Read aloud the prophecy Zechariah spoke when his little son John was born in Luke 1:67-79. Now spend some time (again!) laying before the Lord the things you are waiting for Him do in your life.

☐ *Check here when you have filled out your timeline with the new entries from this lesson.*

GOD

INTERTESTAMENTAL PERIOD
400 YEARS
GREEK LANGUAGE
SYNAGOGUES
PEACE
ROADS

46. ZECHARIAH & ELIZABETH
47. JOHN THE BAPTIST

LESSON THIRTY

PRAYER MOMENT

Today in your study you will encounter someone proclaiming, *"For the Word of God will never fail."* Pray, as you begin your lesson, that God's Word will accomplish its work in you today.

BIBLE PASSAGE

Read Luke 1:26-56 and use the space below to record any questions it brings to mind or things you notice.

Consider how this unfolded. Read Gabriel's words and then note how Mary responded.

GABRIEL'S WORDS	MARY'S RESPONSE:
"Greetings favored woman! The Lord is with you! (Vs. 28)	Vs. 29
"Don't be afraid, Mary, for you have found favor with God! You will conceive and give birth to a son, and you will name him Jesus. He will be very great and will be called the Son of the Most High. The Lord God will give Him the throne of his ancestor David. And He will reign over Israel forever; his Kingdom will never end!" (Vs. 30-33)	Vs. 34
"The Holy Spirit will come upon you and the power of the Most High will overshadow you. So the baby to be born will be holy, and He will be called the Son of God. What's more, your relative Elizabeth has become pregnant in her old age! People used to say she was barren, but she has conceived a son and is now in her sixth month. For the word of God will never fail." (Vs. 35-37)	Vs. 38

Go back and look at what Mary asked Gabriel in verse 34. How does it compare to Zechariah's question in verse 18, which we studied yesterday? What do you think the difference was? Why did Gabriel respond with an explanation for Mary, but with a consequence for Zechariah?

Lesson Thirty

There was to be no uncertainty in Mary's mind about what the Lord was in the midst of doing! Look back over Gabriel's words on the previous page and circle all the words which describe this baby.

Look at the progression in **Mary's responses** on the previous page. How would you sum that up?

Mary went from _____ to _____

to _____.

God's revelation gradually unfolded for Mary. And she walked with the Lord, through fear and confusion, and came to submit to His Lordship over her. What a pattern for us to emulate!

Consider your own life. As **God gradually reveals things** to you, do you respond by submitting to His lead in your life? Or do you push back and try to negotiate with Him for a different plan?

In what area of your life is He walking you through this process right now?

List here what the Lord has revealed to you so far about the area you noted above:

Do you know enough yet to discern where specifically He is leading?

How are you currently responding to this lead?

Just as he did for Mary, the Lord wants to use your life for meaningful and eternal purposes. He has amazing and mysterious plans for you and is constantly readying you for the next step. Pause and pray about how He is working in your life, using Mary's words:

"I am the Lord's servant. May everything You have said about me come true."

Read again the sweet scene between Mary and her cousin Elizabeth in verses 39-45.

How did this interaction further confirm what the Lord was doing in Mary's life?

Have you talked with any trusted friends about what God is doing in the area of your life noted above? If so, sum up what was said here. If not, list a friend or two you should talk this through with.

Kingdom of God Prophesied 119

Upon realizing the gravity of what the Lord was involving her in, Mary overflowed with praise. Faithful Jews had been watching and waiting over a 400 year period for this time to come, and now Mary was standing at the brink of a new era – the **Messiah** was coming!

PRAYER MOMENT

Mary's prayer of praise which ends this chapter offers us a pattern we can use to pray.

Fill in the following as you pray through these words today:

> "Oh, how my soul praises the Lord. How my spirit rejoices in God my Savior!
> For he **took notice** of me.
> (Praise the Lord that He sees and **takes notice** of you and your situation!)

_____

_____

> For the Mighty One is holy, and He has done **great** things for me.
> He shows mercy from generation to generation to all who fear Him.
> His mighty arm has done **tremendous** things!
> (What **great** and **tremendous** things have you seen Him do?)

_____

_____

> He has scattered the proud and haughty ones.
> He has brought down princes from their thrones and exalted the humble.
> He has filled the hungry with good things and sent the rich away with empty hands.
> He has helped His servant Israel and remembered to be merciful.
> For He made this **promise** to our ancestors, to Abraham and his children forever."
> (Praise the Lord for **fulfilling what He promised**, bringing us the Messiah!)

_____

_____

KINGDOM OF GOD
PRESENT

LESSON THIRTY-ONE

PRAYER MOMENT

"My thoughts are nothing like your thoughts," says the LORD.
"And my ways are far beyond anything you could imagine. For just as the heavens are higher than the earth,
so my ways are higher than your ways and my thoughts higher than your thoughts."
Isaiah 55:8-9

As you open your study today, praise the Lord for His ideas and plans that are far better than what we could ever come up with!

Ponder this question: If you were God, how would you have sent your Son to earth? Jot your thoughts here:

BIBLE PASSAGE

Read Luke 2:1-52 and use the space below to record any questions it brings to mind or things you notice.

The way the Lord would *send* His Son, and then *use* His Son, demonstrates that His values are not like ours. Notice all of the unusual facets of the way God sent Jesus (verses 1-7). List here what you see:

What descriptive words could be used for this scene?

This event would not remain quiet and unobtrusive for long. The Lord would supernaturally draw attention to this earth-shattering, earth-saving event. Read verses 8-18 to see how He did this.

So, how did the Lord feel about this event? When we read the angel's proclamation to the shepherds (vs. 10-11) we can understand the Lord's heart about this. After all, how had the angel gained this insight? Surely from the Lord Himself.

"I bring you good news that will bring great joy to all people.
The Savior, yes, the Messiah, the Lord – has been born today in Bethlehem, the city of David!"

Notice three names are given to describe this baby. Circle them in the verse on the previous page.

What do you think is conveyed by each name:

Savior   **Messiah**   **Lord**

What did the shepherds do immediately upon hearing the angels' announcement? (vs. 15-16)

What did the shepherds do after seeing Jesus? (vs. 17-20)

The next scene we encounter in Luke 2 is an interesting one. Since we have very few snapshots of Jesus' childhood given in Scripture, each one is worth examining. This one occurred eight days after Jesus was born. Understand that the law required that Mary and Joseph go to the temple to have Jesus circumcised, and also to make the sacrifice required after the birth of a child. Throughout His life, Jesus would fulfill the requirements of the law in every way, and this was part of it.

Given the glory-filled scene with the shepherds, Mary and Joseph may have expected their appearance at the temple to be met with great celebration. After all, this was the *temple* – how would the priests react to their Messiah?! Sadly, it appears that the priests didn't notice. Maybe they and their forefathers had lost their anticipation over the 400-year wait. Or perhaps Jesus had come on the scene too quietly, in too much of an unexpected, unassuming way.

There were, however, two who did notice: **Simeon and Anna**.

	SIMEON	ANNA
How is this person described?	Vs. 25-26	Vs. 36-37
How did he/she get to the temple?	Vs. 27	Vs. 37
How did he/she respond to the sight of Jesus?	Vs. 28	Vs. 38
What does this person say about Jesus?	Vs. 30-32	Vs. 38 (What can you infer that she said?)

Lesson Thirty-One

How do you imagine Mary and Joseph felt when they left the temple that day?

From here, we fast forward 12 years to view another snapshot of Jesus' childhood in verses 41-52. As was their custom, Mary and Joseph, along with a throng of family and friends, made their annual pilgrimage to Jerusalem to celebrate the Passover festival.

Jesus lags behind unnoticed when His parents leave. Why (vs. 46)?

What explanation does Jesus give (vs. 49)?

Jesus' first visit to the temple had been missed by the temple leaders. He wanted to make sure they didn't remain in the dark. He had come – the Light of the World, and he wanted to open their eyes!

In today's lesson we saw varied responses to the arrival of Jesus. Can you identify with any of the individuals in our reading:

The <u>temple teachers</u> were unclear about who Jesus really was, although they had been around religion all of their lives. They listened and considered what He said. They needed to be taught, yes, but what they needed even more was a personal encounter with Jesus. Is that where you are today?

The <u>shepherds</u> heard a little about Jesus, and then rushed to find out more. They wanted to personally see the Messiah, and they dropped everything to find Him. Afterward, they went back to their work, but were forever changed. Are you at a place where you are pursuing Jesus like that? Trying to find out everything you can?

<u>Simeon and Anna</u> understood with clarity who Jesus was. They had spent their lives seeking God and waiting for the Messiah. When Jesus came on the scene, they praised God and spoke out about who Jesus was. Do you have that level of conviction about Jesus? Are you confident enough to speak out about Him?

PRAYER MOMENT

Consider where your encounter with Jesus has taken you. Then journal a prayer below, asking God to move you forward in your relationship with Christ.

☐ *Check here when you have filled out your timeline with the new entries from this lesson.*

BIBLICAL THEME:
THE KINGDOM OF GOD

With the advent of Jesus, we arrive at an important transition in Biblical history. Remember, the people of God waited many years for God's promised Messiah to come on the scene during the period we have called "The Kingdom of God Prophesied." But, as we turn the page to the New Testament, the Messiah has arrived on the scene! The Lord is *present* with His people in the person of Jesus.

So, let's revisit our theme: the **KINGDOM OF GOD**, focusing this time on how Jesus' life was distinct in these areas.

God's _____

in God's _____

under God's _____

enjoying God's _____

God's **PEOPLE:** In what way is Jesus "God's person?"

God's **PLACE:** Is Jesus in the place where God intended Him to be?

God's **RULE:** How is Jesus following the lead of the Lord? Is Jesus obeying Him?

God's **BLESSING:** Is Jesus enjoying God's blessing? How do we see that?

Is God's blessing overflowing from Jesus' life onto others?

As we watch Jesus' life unfold in the upcoming pages, keep an eye out for the way He lived. All that God had planned for mankind – for them to be His people, living in the place He had prepared for them, submitting to His rule, and enjoying His blessing – we see Jesus do perfectly. Where Adam fell short, and where we also fail, Jesus succeeds. God's kingdom comes to earth when Jesus comes on the scene; the **Kingdom of God is <u>present</u>**.

☐ *Check here when you have written "Kingdom of God Present" in Oval F on your Timeline.*

LESSON THIRTY-TWO

> ## PRAYER MOMENT
>
> How do you think God the Father would describe Jesus? In prayer, consider that as you open your study today.
>
> ## BIBLE PASSAGE
>
> Read Matthew 3:13-4:11 and use the space below to record any questions it brings to mind or things you notice.

What has been your exposure to the idea of baptism? What do you understand it to represent?

You are probably as confused as John was about why Jesus would need to be baptized. You may be even more confused when you understand this:

In Matthew 3:6 John baptized people after they did what? Matthew 3:11 gives further details. John baptized people who…

As John came on the scene calling people to baptism, he was introducing a shocking and outrageous thought to them. The Jews had come to depend on their heritage to gain them favor with God. So, it created quite a stir when John said, "It's not enough just to be in Abraham's line. There is a sin problem here, people!"

Remember, John's role was to <u>prepare</u> the people for the Messiah - for Jesus the Savior. Why would they need a Savior if they were unaware of their need to be saved? It was essential for them to *face* the problem of the sin which separated them from the perfect God.

So, now you understand baptism signifies a person's confession of sin, repentance from that sin, and their turning to God. But the question remains: Why was *Jesus* baptized?

Verse 15 provides Jesus' answer to that question. What does He say?

To "fulfill all righteousness" Jesus would obey God the Father in every way throughout His life. Here God had instituted the new practice of baptism for His people, so Jesus would submit to this new requirement as well. Baptism would come to serve as a sign of the new covenant being established in Jesus, so it was fitting for Jesus for Jesus to come under that sign.

Theologian R. C. Sproul explains it this way:

"It was necessary for Jesus to obey every detail of every law that was imposed upon the people of God, and God had now imposed a new requirement. And though Jesus had no sin of his own, to fulfill all righteousness, He submits to the Baptism of John."

This chapter concludes with God's verbal approval of His Son. How amazing it must have been to hear the Father's voice boom from heaven that day.

Transcribe what God said in verse 17 here, thinking through the gravity of each word as you write.

It sounds as if all will be well now… And then we open up to Matthew 4. The Holy Spirit *leads* Jesus out into the wilderness for what purpose? (Matthew 4:1) _____

Being the Lord's "Dearly Loved Son" did not exempt Jesus from facing temptation. In fact, it was essential for Jesus to identify with us in <u>all</u> of our human predicament. To face temptation just the same as Adam did in Genesis 3. Just the same as you do today. You *are* God's dearly loved child, but the brokenness and temptation in this world is a reality you must contend with as well.

So, Satan schemes. And he waits. Until he finds an opportune time.

In what condition does Satan find Jesus (Vs. 2)?

TEMPTATION ONE:

Read Matthew 4:1-4. In the space above draw a simple sketch to represent the temptation Satan presented here.

In verse 3 Satan opens with the words "*If* you are the Son of God." What had God just established in Matthew 3:17?

Think back to the beginning of our study when we examined the Fall of Adam and Eve. Rewrite in the box below what you wrote in the box at the bottom of page 16.

Here again Satan was up to the same old trick. God told Jesus who He was, and now Satan was attempting to introduce doubt about this truth!

Lesson Thirty-Two

In your life, realize that Satan is always trying to cause you to doubt the good and true things God says about you. Can you think of how you have experienced that personally?

What lies would Satan like you to believe about yourself?

How does Jesus respond to Satan's temptation?

In this first interaction, Jesus is setting the ground rules – the success principle for His life.

Jesus would live by: _____ _____ that comes from the _____ _____ _____.
(Vs. 4)

If life comes by living according to God's word, what would the opposite of this principle be?

People will die by: _____ every word that comes from the mouth of God.

TEMPTATION TWO:

Read Matthew 4:5-7. In the space above draw a simple sketch to represent the temptation Satan presented here.

What do you notice here that is the same as Temptation #1, and what is different?

Same:

Different:

How did Jesus respond?

Jesus was establishing another ruling principle for His life: He would trust God's promises, and not manipulate situations to prove God could keep them. He knew God's word to be true and trustworthy.

TEMPTATION THREE:

Read Matthew 4:8-10. Again draw a simple sketch to represent the temptation Satan presented here.

If you know the end of the story, you can see that Satan was offering Jesus a shortcut:

"Get exaltation without _____."

What is the ruling principle Jesus established here (vs. 10)?

SATAN TEMPTED JESUS...	JESUS WOULD ONE DAY...
"Make bread!"	Make bread... for the multitudes. (Matt. 14 & 15)
"Throw your life down!"	Lay His life down... on the cross. (John 10:17-18)
"Get the kingdoms of the world!"	Get the kingdoms of the world... when every knee will bow to Him. (Phil. 2:8-11)

Don't miss this fact: Satan doesn't waste his attacks. The enemy attacks in areas which matter. Areas in which Jesus bears great fruit when He does them **at the right time, in the right place, and in obedience to His Father.**

What does that tell you about the areas in which Satan attacks you?

PRAYER MOMENT

It is so vital for us to be wise to the enemy's schemes. Go back through today's lesson and list below what you have learned from watching Jesus contend with Satan.

Now pray that you will have wisdom when you personally contend with Satan's schemes.

☐ Check here when you have filled out your timeline with the new entries from this lesson.

LESSON THIRTY-THREE

PRAYER MOMENT

*Jesus said, "I have come that they may have life, and have it **to the full**."*
John 10:10

Pray that you will see today how Jesus came to provide a ***rich*** and ***satisfying*** life to those who would follow Him.

BIBLE PASSAGE

Read Matthew 5:1-26 and use the space below to record any questions it brings to mind or things you notice.

Are you familiar with either of the following quotes?

"The only thing we have to fear is fear itself."
"Ask not what your country can do for you; ask what you can do for your country."

You have most likely heard these sentences before. The first is a statement made in Franklin D. Roosevelt's inaugural address in 1933, and the second is an excerpt from John F. Kennedy's inaugural address given in 1961. An inauguration **marks the launch** of a major public leader's term of office, and the speech which is given **advises the people of his intentions** as a leader.

The Scripture before us today is like an inaugural address signifying the beginning of Jesus' public ministry. On this day Jesus sat before the gathered crowd and gave His inaugural address: the Sermon on the Mount. Even if your exposure to Scripture is limited, you'll recognize many of the statements in this section. As is the case with the presidential quotes, these words from Jesus encapsulate **who He was and how He would lead**.

So where does Jesus begin? With **BLESSING**! His rule would be *marked* with *blessing*.

Matthew 5:1-12 – Blessing for Followers

Verse	Who? Write the word used in the verse.	Synonym Write a synonym for the word.	End Result How does God meet these people with blessing?
3			
4			

130 Finding Your Way

5		
6		
7		
8		
9		
10		
11-12		

All of the people in these verses have what in common?

Which of these qualities don't come easily for you?

In these blessing-statements ("Beatitudes") Jesus is calling the people to be different from the surrounding world. In the next section Jesus reiterates the distinctiveness which should mark His followers, focusing on the *blessing they bring to the world* around them.

Matthew 5:13-16 — Blessing from Followers...

YOU ARE the _____ (vs. 13)

What does salt do?

What would negate its impact?

Sum it up: **"Followers of Jesus bless the world by _____."**

YOU ARE the _____ (vs. 14-15)

What does light do?

What would negate its impact?

Sum it up: **"Followers of Jesus bless the world by _____."**

GOD

INTERTESTAMENTAL PERIOD
400 YEARS
GREEK LANGUAGE
SYNAGOGUES
PEACE
ROADS

ZECHARIAH & ELIZABETH
JOHN THE BAPTIST
MARY & JOSEPH

JESUS' BIRTH
JESUS' BAPTISM
JESUS' TEMPTATION
52. SERMON ON THE MOUNT

Kingdom of God
PRESENT

Lesson Thirty-Three

> What would it look like for you to function as salt and light in *your* world? What makes this difficult for you?

Remember where we are in tracing our Kingdom of God theme…

Kingdom of God _____

All of history was leading up to this point when **Jesus the <u>King</u> would actually be <u>present</u> with His people** and would **lead them into His kingdom.** But when He came, He was not what the people expected. His quiet birth, His humble ways, His gentle demeanor – the people weren't sure what to make of it. And then He began to teach. His kingdom values seemed upside down. Was He doing away with all that had come before - all that the law and the prophets (the Old Testament Scriptures) had taught them?

Knowing that this was swirling around in their minds, Jesus answered these questions for them.

"I did not come to _____ the law and prophets,

I came to _____ their purpose."

Matthew 5:17-18

That which men and women had been unable to do (be God's people, dwelling in His place, willingly accepting His rule, basking in His blessing) Christ fully did. Jesus had not come to <u>abolish</u> all that had come before in the Scriptures, but to <u>accomplish</u> it!

PRAYER MOMENT

Ponder the following in prayer:

The Law detailed God's requirements, yet we have seen throughout our study that the Jews fell miserably short time after time. Into this hopeless situation the prophets spoke, bringing promise of a coming Messiah who would perfectly obey God, offer forgiveness, and be their salvation. He would make up for their lack of obedience, cleanse their sin, and give them access to God. We, too, are unable to obey God's law perfectly; Jesus had to do it for us.

Have you allowed Jesus to accomplish for you what you cannot do on your own?

→ If you have, you are a follower of Jesus. Pray now that you will **be the salt and light** this world urgently needs.

→ If you have not, pray about **what is holding you back** from allowing Jesus to do for you what you cannot do.

☐ *Check here when you have filled out your timeline with the new entries from this lesson.*

LESSON THIRTY-FOUR

PRAYER MOMENT

Today, what are some of the needs facing you in your life and the lives of those around you?

Lay these before the Lord in prayer as you open your study today.

BIBLE PASSAGE

Read John 6:1-15 and use the space below to record any questions it brings to mind or things you notice.

A huge crowd had spontaneously assembled on that day. What drew them (vs. 2)?

Jesus saw the crowd and asked Philip, one of His disciples, a question (vs. 5). What was Jesus trying to draw to Philip's attention?

Jesus had a unique ability to see beyond the surface to the needs within. On another day, He was faced with a different crowd and "had **compassion** on them, because they were like sheep without a shepherd, so He began teaching them many things." (Mark 6:34)

Compassion. That is what marked Jesus' response. Compassion for a crowd who needed to be taught. Compassion for a crowd who needed to be fed. And that compassion moved Him to act. Whether confusion or hunger, Jesus wanted to meet the need.

In contrast, we are often overwhelmed by the enormity of the needs we see and are reticent to act.

In verse 7, what does Philip point out?

But we know that Jesus "was testing Philip" (vs. 6). What was the test?

Kingdom of God Present 133

Lesson Thirty-Four

Can you identify with what Philip was feeling? In this broken world we, too, are faced with many needs which seem too big for us to do anything about. Our resources are terribly inadequate to solve the problem. Reflect on the things you listed in the "Prayer Moment" at the beginning of the lesson.

Do you feel you don't have the resources which are needed to meet those needs? How so?

In the scene we are studying, it seemed almost comical how miniscule the resources were in the face of this huge crowd. Andrew, another of Jesus' disciples sums it up in verse 9:

"_____ a young boy here with five barley loaves and two fish.

But _____ with this huge crowd?"

When we view the great needs around us don't we look at our resources the same way?

<u>There is</u> this small resource I have….<u>but what good is that</u> with this huge need?

But a miracle was about to unfold in this story! Look how it happens in verses 10-13.

List all the things which you think are crucial to this miracle:

The pattern on display in this account is similar to the pattern we saw in the story of Abraham and Sarah. (Glance back to page 27 to refresh your memory, looking at the second equation in the middle of the page.)

Here is the pattern demonstrated in the feeding of the 5,000:

ENORMOUS NEED + **THEIR INABILITY TO MEET THEIR NEED** + **OFFER THE LITTLE THEY HAVE** + **GOD MEETS THE NEED (MIRACULOUS)** = **BLESSING FOR MANY**

What reasons could the boy have given to *not* share the little he had?

What if the boy had refused to share? What would have been missed (vs. 14)?

The same is true in your life. What if you don't use the little resource you have to touch the needs around you?

The need in your friend's broken heart?
The need in your wife's anxious mind?
The need in your child's faltering self-worth?
The need in your husband's discouraged demeanor?
The need in the wounded and hurting world which surrounds you?

Yet, as was the case for Philip, Jesus has drawn your attention to the needs around you. Your heart is moved with compassion, and you wish you could do something.

Look again at the steps you listed on the previous page which were crucial to the unfolding of the miracle. These are the keys for you also.

PRAYER MOMENT

Choose one of the needs you listed at the beginning of this lesson and journal a prayer below, following the steps which you listed from the miracle of the loaves and fishes. Ask the Lord to allow you to do your part to touch that need as you offer your resources, insufficient though they may seem.

☐ *Check here when you have filled out your timeline with the new entries from this lesson.*

GOD

INTERTESTAMENTAL PERIOD
400 YEARS
GREEK LANGUAGE
SYNAGOGUES
PEACE
ROADS

ZECHARIAH & ELIZABETH
JOHN THE BAPTIST
MARY & JOSEPH

JESUS' BIRTH
JESUS' BAPTISM
JESUS' TEMPTATION
SERMON ON THE MOUNT

JESUS' MIRACLES INCLUDING:
53. FEEDING 5,000

Kingdom of God
PRESENT

LESSON THIRTY-FIVE

PRAYER MOMENT

Pray that you will understand the truth of this verse as you study today:

"Without vision (redemptive revelation of God and His word), the people perish."
Proverbs 29:18a

Write a short explanation of these commonly-used phrases:

"Blinding light"

"Blind as a bat"

"Turn a blind eye toward"

"He has a blind spot"

Sight is important to us – so important that it even shows up in our catch phrases. Taste, hearing, smell... most people would rather lose any sense other than their sight. What a struggle it must be to go through life without sight, straining along, trying to compensate with other senses.

This is where our story begins today - with the life of a man who had been in darkness since birth, blind throughout his whole life. Miraculously his eyes were opened by Jesus. Our story ends, ironically, in the same place, with several others who were also unable to see. Though given the opportunity to have their blindness lifted, they preferred the darkness they lived in because it felt familiar and safe. How tragic.

Why is sight such an important sense for us? What are all the ways it benefits us?

BIBLE PASSAGE

Read John 9:1-41 and use the space below to record any questions it brings to mind or things you notice.

What question did the disciples ask (Vs. 2)?

Isn't this always what we ask when we see pain in the world: "Why, Lord?" What did the disciples suggest as possible answers to the question?

What answer did Jesus give (Vs. 3)?

Here is Jesus' explanation in the New International Version:

> "…this happened so that the work of God might be displayed in his life." (Vs. 3b)

It is amazing to realize that whatever the specific cause of the pain we experience in this world, it is always an opportunity for the Lord to be glorified. These places of brokenness are opportunities for God to work and for the power of God to be seen. It is true that I am often the cause of my own pain – poor decisions, compromise, sin – I foolishly invite brokenness into my life. In other instances, the sin of others spills over and affects my life. Still other times, my life is touched by the diffused dysfunction of a world which is itself broken - things just don't work in the perfect way in which they were originally created. I can get stuck on the "Why?" or I can say "What now?" and get about **seeing the power of God manifest** in these areas.

This passage is all about seeing…

        Seeing who <u>Jesus</u> is   &   Seeing who <u>we</u> are

As this story opens, Jesus identifies Himself with an intriguing title:

"I am _____ (vs. 5).

Thinking about how light affects vision, what do you think Jesus meant when he used this title for Himself?

Read again verses 6-9 and summarize what happened.

When they saw him healed, the neighbors and others who knew this man doubted his identity. However, he kept saying "Yes, I am the same one!" Who did this man know himself to be?

This man was clear on his identity – he was the blind beggar. He didn't candy coat it, but fully admitted his broken neediness. As the story progressed, the beggar gradually came to see who Jesus was with greater clarity.

GOD

INTERTESTAMENTAL PERIOD
400 YEARS
GREEK LANGUAGE
SYNAGOGUES
PEACE
ROADS

ZECHARIAH & ELIZABETH
JOHN THE BAPTIST
MARY & JOSEPH

JESUS' BIRTH
JESUS' BAPTISM
JESUS' TEMPTATION
SERMON ON THE MOUNT

JESUS' MIRACLES
INCLUDING:
FEEDING 5,000

54. HEALING BLIND MAN

Kingdom of God
PRESENT

Lesson Thirty-Five

This blind beggar's eyes were being slowly opened to who Jesus is.

Vs. 11	"the _____ they call _____"
Vs. 17	"he must be a _____"
Vs. 25	"a healer"
Vs. 27	"a disciple-maker"
Vs. 33	"from God"
Vs. 35-37	"Son of _____"
Vs. 38	"_____, I believe"

Look back over this list and notice the progressive revelation which unfolded.

Have you experienced a gradual revelation of Jesus in your life? How would you trace your progressive understanding of who Jesus is?

Our understanding of **who Jesus is** walks side by side with our understanding of **who we are**.

The man saw Jesus as...
...from God...
...the healer...
...the Son of Man...
...the Lord...
He saw clearly **who Jesus was**.

Over and over again the man proclaims...

"I am the blind beggar."

...and he saw clearly **who he was**.

In contrast, the Pharisees saw neither. The Pharisees suffered from a fatal case of spiritual blindness. Remember at the beginning of this lesson when you defined what it means to have a "blind spot"? Look back and see what you wrote. This is similar to how their spiritual blindness manifested itself.

Verse 34 gives us a glimpse of their thinking. What did they say, and what does that demonstrate?

They were unwilling to see who they were, and they were **unwilling to see who Jesus was**. Look back through the passage and note who they accused Jesus of being (vs. 13-34).

Jesus proclaimed, *"I entered this world to render judgement – to give sight to the blind and to show those who think they see that they are blind."* (vs. 39) He was poised and ready to help those who would admit their need, yet the Pharisees refused His help, resting instead on their own self-sufficient religiosity.

The key moment for the blind beggar unfolds in verse 38. What step does he take?

PRAYER MOMENT

We need to do the same - to go from understanding the facts about who Jesus is, to bowing before Him in worship. Close your study today by worshipping Jesus for who you know Him to be. Then ask for your eyes to be opened even more so that you may know Him more fully.

☐ *Check here when you have filled out your timeline with the new entries from this lesson.*

LESSON THIRTY-SIX

> ## PRAYER MOMENT
>
> Reflect on the various homes where you have lived and what led you to move each time. Thank the Lord for what you learned in the good times and the hard times at each place.

Home. It was the place that most represented home to me. And when I drove down the descending driveway that clear fall day, I knew I was doing so for the last time in my life. My parents had sold the home where I had grown up for my first 23 years, and where I had visited them for the next 23. They were leaving there to move into my home. As I bumped along the gravelly terrain, my eyes brimming with tears, I realized that I would never again have a place that felt quite like this. So much history. So many memories. A place where I was noticed and listened to and understood. A place where someone always slowed down for me. Where I was never an inconvenience, nor disinteresting. A place where I learned who the Lord is, and learned who I am, in safety and peace. The tears streaming, I thanked the Lord for this uncommon gift. And I set my heart to make my home this for others - my kids, my husband, my parents, my nieces and nephews, friends and family. Because we all, deep down, long for somewhere that feels like home.

What place in your life most felt like **home** to you? What made it feel that way?

Keep your eyes open as you read today, looking for the references to **"home"** in this chapter of Scripture.

> ## BIBLE PASSAGE
>
> Read John 14:1-31 and use the space below to record any questions it brings to mind or things you notice.

Jesus is "speaking our language" when He talks in this passage about His Father's home.

What place is He actually talking about in verses 1-3? _____

There are several pieces of good news that Jesus gives about this heavenly home in these verses. List them and put a star by the one that is most significant to you.

In verse 5 Thomas is confused about both the destination and the route to this destination. Sum up what he is asking.

Kingdom of God Present 139

Lesson Thirty-Six

Thomas's confusion is understandable. Jesus is talking about a place so real that it has rooms which need preparation. However, the way to get there doesn't involve certain roads or specific transportation modes. The way to get there involves a person. This person is the way, the route, the means to get to heaven.

Who is "the way"? (vs. 6) _____

Gradually, Jesus is revealing Himself to these people who were His followers. But as He spoke, it all seemed so mysterious and confusing. What exactly was He getting at? Who did He claim to be? Verses 6-13 shed light on this.

From these verses, list all the things Jesus and God the Father share:

Vs. 6 -

Vs. 7 -

Vs. 9 -

Vs. 10 -

Vs. 13 -

The Father and the Son have an exquisite communion, and they invite you into their fellowship, into their activity. Amazing! But why? Because that is what God created man for in the first place - to share in His community, to be a part of His family. The Father overflows with love and wants children to share it with. This is one Father who is *always* eager to adopt!

And being in the family produces a family resemblance. His children come to look like Him, and come to do the same things which God the Father and Jesus are already doing.

What does verse 12 say God's children will do?

When we are out and about, doing God's work, we have the special privilege of asking the Father for things. What caveats are given about what we can ask for (vs. 13-14)?

"You can ask for anything _____, and I will do it,

so that the _____.

Yes, ask me for anything _____, and I will do it!"

What do you think this means?

140 Finding Your Way

Does this all sound a little daunting? How can you go out and join the Father in His work? And how can you know what types of things to ask Him for? It would be hopeless if you were left to figure it all out on your own, but you're not.

Read verses 15-26 and list all the descriptive terms given for the Helper who God provides.

Verse 17 specifies that this Helper, the Holy Spirit, "lives _____ you now and later will be _____ you."

Verse 23 adds that Jesus and the Father will "come and _____ with each of them (those who are God's adopted children)."

We will see in the upcoming lessons how all of this came to fruition. For now, bask in the fact that **God Himself makes His home in those who come to Him for salvation**. The Father knows how we yearn for the feeling that only "home" can give us. He promises we will experience it with Him in His presence one day. But **for now, He is at home here within us**. That is a marvel!

PRAYER MOMENT

Lay before the Lord in prayer your need for "home" in your life. Ask Him to meet you there, and to make you aware of His presence.

LESSON THIRTY-SEVEN

PRAYER MOMENT

*"But He was pierced for our rebellion, crushed for our sins.
He was beaten so we could be whole. He was whipped so we could be healed."*
Isaiah 53:5

As you begin your study today, thank the Lord for all that Jesus went through to provide salvation for YOU.

BIBLE PASSAGE

Read Mark 15:1-47 and use the space below to record any questions it brings to mind or things you notice.

Our salvation is a marvel. The creator of the universe has such devotion to the people He made that He would deploy His own Son to earth in order to save them. Astonishing! And Jesus would have to suffer immensely to accomplish this salvation for us:

Suffer being wrongly accused.
Suffer being mocked and taunted.
Suffer being beaten and spit on.
Suffer the torture of death on a cross.

All to ultimately suffer the punishment which mankind earned through its sin: separation from God.

Way ahead of time, the Lord told us this is what it would take. Throughout the Old Testament, as God revealed Himself, hints were being given about the Savior to come. Beginning in Genesis, these "Messianic Prophecies" give details about how it would happen. There are over a hundred of these hints, which cover everything from His genealogy, to where He would be born, to how He would come on the scene, to how He would die. You see, God wanted us to be really sure. We are staking our eternity on His solution to our sin problem. God wanted to make it entirely clear that Jesus is, indeed, the One He had promised to save us.

Pilate hit upon the key question in Mark 15:2. What did he ask?

How did Jesus respond to this question (vs. 2)?

How did the religious leaders respond to Jesus being called the "**King of the Jews**" (vs. 9-13)?

How did the Roman soldiers respond to Jesus being called the "**King of the Jews**" (vs. 16-19)?

This is the key question for you, too: Is Jesus the **King of the Jews, the Messiah** who was promised? And if so, how then will <u>you</u> respond to Him?

Let's look at today's reading with that question in mind: **"Is Jesus the King of the Jews?"** Fill in the following to assemble an answer to that question.

THE MESSIAH WILL…	PROPHECY FORETOLD Underline what these Old Testament verses say will be true about the Messiah	PROPHECY FULFILLED Write how this is fulfilled in Jesus' life in these New Testament verses
…be tried & condemned.	"Unjustly condemned, He was led away. No one cared that he died without descendants, that His life was cut short in midstream…" Isaiah 53:8	Mark 15:3-4, 12-15
…be silent before His accusers.	"Malicious witnesses testify against me, they accuse me of crimes I know nothing about." Psalm 35:11 "He was oppressed and treated harshly, yet he never said a word. He was led like a lamb to the slaughter, and as a sheep is silent before the shearers, he did not open his mouth." Isaiah 53:7-8a	Mark 15:3-5
…be mocked & tortured.	"Everyone who sees me mocks me. They sneer and shake their heads, saying, "Is this the One who relies on the Lord? Then let the Lord save him! If the Lord loves him so much, let the Lord rescue him." Psalm 22:7-8	Mark 15:16-18, 31-32
…be beaten & spit on.	"I offered my back to those who beat me, and my cheeks to those who pulled out my beard. I do not hide my face from mockery and spitting." Isaiah 50:6	Mark 15:19
…be nailed to a cross.	"My enemies surround me like a pack of dogs, an evil gang closes in on me. They have pierced my hands and feet." Psalm 22:16	Mark 15:24
…suffer with sinners.	"I will give Him the honors of One who is mighty and great, because He exposed Himself to death. He was counted among those who were sinners." Isaiah 53:12a	Mark 15:27
…have people gamble for His clothes.	"They divide my garments among themselves. They cast lots for my clothing." Psalm 22:18	Mark 15:24
…be buried in the tomb of a wealthy man.	"He had done no wrong and had never deceived anyone. But he was buried like a criminal; he was put in a rich man's grave." Isaiah 53:9	Mark 15:43

Lesson Thirty-Seven

PRAYER MOMENT

As we close, let's revisit the verse you prayed through as you opened your lesson today:

"But He was pierced through for our transgressions,
He was crushed for our iniquities:
The chastening for our well-being fell upon Him,
and by His scourging we are healed."
Isaiah 53:5

In the space below, rewrite this verse, replacing "our" with "my," and "we" with "I":

Among the mocking and sneering voices at the foot of the cross stood one who could see beyond what was visible. He saw into the supernatural reality on the cross before them.

What does the Roman officer conclude about Jesus in Mark 15:39?

Jesus is the King of the Jews, the Son of God, the promised Messiah who came to die for you.

The priests wanted to kill Him.
The soldiers mocked Him.
But the Roman officer worshipped Him as the Son of God.

Like the priests, the soldiers, and the Roman officer, *you* must decide how *you* will respond to Him.

Below, write a prayer, putting into words your response to Jesus:

☐ *Check here when you have filled out your timeline with the new entries from this lesson.*

LESSON THIRTY-EIGHT

PRAYER MOMENT

If you know this hymn, sing it out to the Lord in prayer. (If not, pray through these words.)

*"Christ the Lord is risen today, Alleluia. Sons of men and angels say, Alleluia.
Raise your joys and triumphs high, Alleluia. Sing, ye heavens, and earth reply, Alleluia."*
(Charles Wesley, Hymn for Easter Day, 1793)

What are some Easter memories from your childhood?

As you read the resurrection story today, consider what Easter memories these characters collected through what they experienced. What would have been Jesus' memories of Easter? How about the women in the story? And how about the disciples? They each experienced this event from differing vantage points, yet they all realized the gravity of what had occurred and were forever changed because of it.

BIBLE PASSAGE

Read Luke 24:1-12 and use the space below to record any questions it brings to mind or things you notice.

THE WOMEN

List the women who were involved (Vs. 10).

_____ _____ _____

They Looked...

Vs. 5 "Why are you looking **among the dead** for someone **who is living**?

Vs. 6 "He _____. He _____."

They Puzzled...

What do you think they imagined had happened to Jesus' body?

Kingdom of God Present 145

Lesson Thirty-Eight

They Remembered...

In verse 6 the angels say, "Remember what Jesus told you back in Galilee..."

List what Jesus had told them before His death in the following verses:

Mark 8:31

Mark 9:30-32

Matthew 20:17-19

Put a check mark by the parts of Jesus' prophecy which were fulfilled.

They Rushed...

Read Luke 24:8-11 and picture the scene. The women responded to this realization with such feverish excitement that their message sounded like gibberish. Somehow, I can understand that the men found it difficult to track with them when they showed up with this announcement. These men had to see it with their own eyes. Understandable.

PETER

He jumped... He ran... He stooped... He peered... He saw...

With desperate eagerness, in verse 12 Peter dashed to the tomb. What do you imagine he saw? Draw it below.

He wondered...

In the same way the women puzzled over what they saw, Peter wonders "What has happened here?" And the Lord gives him the answer.

In John 21:1-14 how does Peter discover the truth of the resurrection for himself?

Everything changed for these people when they discovered one fact:

THE TOMB DID NOT HOLD JESUS!

Why is Jesus' resurrection so important?

146 Finding Your Way

If Jesus had not been raised from the dead, the story would have ended at the grave. The disciples would have remained cowering and hiding, humiliated that they had followed a defeated teacher.

But Jesus was alive again! This meant that nothing, not even death - the worst thing this world could dish out - was stronger than Jesus. He had fulfilled all that He promised. He indeed was the Messiah, the Son of God. And He was qualified to be their Savior.

PRAYER MOMENT

"What we believe is this: If we get included in Christ's sin-conquering death, we also get included in His life-saving resurrection. We know that when Jesus was raised from the dead it was a signal of the end of death-as-the-end. Never again will death have the last word. When Jesus died, He took sin down with Him, but alive He brings God down to us."
Romans 6:7-11 MSG

Below write a prayer, reflecting on what strikes you today about the resurrection of Jesus:

☐ *Check here when you have filled out your timeline with the new entries from this lesson.*

LESSON THIRTY-NINE

PRAYER MOMENT

"But when the Father sends the Advocate as my representative—that is, the Holy Spirit — He will <u>teach</u> you everything and will <u>remind</u> you of everything I have told you."
John 14:26

Ask the Holy Spirit to <u>teach</u> you today as you study, and then continually <u>remind</u> you of what you have learned.

As we turn the page in our study, we open to a new book of the Bible: Acts. And in doing so we move from studying the **life of Jesus** to studying the **lives of the first Christians**. The book of Acts, also known as "the Acts of the Apostles," chronicles what transpired in the fledgling church right after Jesus left them to return to heaven. How would they survive when all they had known was Jesus walking among them? What would this new experience of being a Christ-follower look like? What would characterize them as a group?

What unique struggles do you imagine they faced?

BIBLE PASSAGE

Read Acts 1:1-11 and use the space below to record any questions it brings to mind or things you notice.

Verse 1 begins, "In my first book..." Don't pass by that opening phrase without noticing it. Whoever wrote this book of Acts wrote something else. Curious about who this is? And what else he wrote? You may be able to find these answers in the Bible you're using. Many Bibles include an introduction at the beginning of each book which gives extra details, such as who the author is. (If your Bible doesn't provide this, do a quick search online to find the answer.)

Who wrote Acts? _____ What other book did he write? _____

According to Acts 1:1-3, what two things was Jesus doing during those 40 days after His resurrection when He appeared to His apostles and others?

1. _____

2. _____

148 Finding Your Way

Knowing this is a continuation of the Gospel of Luke, let's glance back at where that book left off in the story. In Luke 24:44-49 Jesus talks about several things, some of which had been fulfilled at that point, and some of which had yet to be fulfilled. Detail this below:

These things had already happened:	These things had not yet occurred:

Understand that the promise of the Holy Spirit coming to live in them must have been a shocker!

Throughout Old Testament times, the Spirit came upon <u>certain people</u> for a <u>limited time</u> for a <u>specific assignment</u>.

Jesus was promising to <u>all believers</u> a <u>permanent indwelling</u> of the Spirit for a <u>lifelong mission</u>. (Remember: He would "make His home in their hearts," as we learned in Lesson 36).

Descriptions of the Holy Spirit – What phrases are used to describe Him in these verses?

Luke 24:49

Acts 1:4

John 14:15-26

Results of the Holy Spirit – What would be the effect of the Holy Spirit coming to dwell in these believers?

Acts 1:8

Luke 24:47-48

Activities of the Holy Spirit – What specific things would the Holy Spirit do in people? (Circle them below.)

"He is the Holy Spirit, who leads into all truth. The world cannot receive Him, because it isn't looking for Him and doesn't recognize Him. But you know Him, because He lives with you now and later will be in you."
John 14:17

"And the Holy Spirit helps us in our weakness. For example, we don't know what God wants us to pray for. But the Holy Spirit prays for us with groanings that cannot be expressed in words."
Romans 8:26-27

GOD

INTERTESTAMENTAL PERIOD
400 YEARS
GREEK LANGUAGE
SYNAGOGUES
PEACE
ROADS

ZECHARIAH & ELIZABETH
JOHN THE BAPTIST
MARY & JOSEPH

JESUS' BIRTH
JESUS' BAPTISM
JESUS' TEMPTATION
SERMON ON THE MOUNT
JESUS' MIRACLES
INCLUDING:
FEEDING 5,000
HEALING BLIND MAN
JESUS' TRIAL BEFORE PILATE
JESUS' CRUCIFICTION
JESUS' RESURRECTION

58. JESUS APPEARS FOR 40 DAYS

59. JESUS' ASCENSION

Kingdom of God
PRESENT

Lesson Thirty-Nine

> "And this hope will not lead to disappointment. For we know how dearly God loves us, because he has given us the Holy Spirit to fill our hearts with His love."
> Romans 5:5

> "And when He (the Holy Spirit) comes, He will convict the world of its sin, and of God's righteousness, and of the coming judgment."
> John 16:8

> "So I say, let the Holy Spirit guide your lives. Then you won't be doing what your sinful nature craves."
> Galatians 5:16

> "But the Holy Spirit produces this kind of fruit in our lives: love, joy, peace, patience, kindness, goodness, faithfulness, gentleness, and self-control. There is no law against these things!"
> Galatians 5:22-23

> "A spiritual gift is given to each of us so we can help each other. To one person the Spirit gives the ability to give wise advice; to another the same Spirit gives a message of special knowledge. The same Spirit gives great faith to another, and to someone else the one Spirit gives the gift of healing. He gives one person the power to perform miracles, and another the ability to prophesy. He gives someone else the ability to discern whether a message is from the Spirit of God or from another spirit. Still another person is given the ability to speak in unknown languages, while another is given the ability to interpret what is being said. It is the one and only Spirit who distributes all these gifts. He alone decides which gift each person should have."
> I Corinthians 12:7-11

Now write a summary statement, detailing what you have learned about the Holy Spirit.

The Holy Spirit...

Jesus would be taken from their presence, but they were comforted with the fact that they would then enjoy the presence of the Holy Spirit.

> "But now I am going away to the One who sent me...in fact, it is best for you that I go away, because if I don't, the Advocate (Holy Spirit) won't come. If I do go away, then I will send Him to you."
> John 16:5,7

With all of this in mind, read again Acts 1: 8-10. What do you imagine they felt at that moment when Jesus ascended into heaven?

PRAYER MOMENT

Sometimes life can make us feel inept, incompetent, unprepared for what we are facing. It is then that we must remember this truth:

> "His divine power has given us **everything we need for life and godliness** through our knowledge of Him."
> II Peter 1:3

The Lord, through His Spirit, equips us far beyond our own abilities!

Now say a prayer, reciting back to the Lord all the things you now know He has given you through His Holy Spirit.

☐ *Check here when you have filled out your timeline with the new entries from this lesson.*

KINGDOM OF GOD
PROCLAIMED

LESSON FORTY

PRAYER MOMENT

On the line below, write a question which has been on your mind today.

_____?

Take a moment to pray about this as you begin your study today.

BIBLE PASSAGE

Read Acts 2:1-41 and use the space below to record any questions it brings to mind or things you notice.

Every day we are constantly asking questions. Questions such as, "What do I need to do today?" "Did I remember to lock the door?" or "How long will this take?"

In our pursuit to bring order to our lives we ask questions. These questions can lead us to wisdom, but only if we ask the *right* questions.

Consider these *right* questions which are asked in Scripture:

"Where are you?" God asked this of Adam and Eve when they hid from Him (Genesis 3:9)
"Who is the Lord?" Pharoah asked this of Moses (Exodus 5:2)
"Who do you say that I am?" Jesus asked this of His disciples (Mark 8:29)
"Are you the King of the Jews?" Pilate asked this of Jesus (Mark 5:2)
"What must I do to be saved?" The Jailer asked this of Paul and Silas (Acts 16:30)

In today's reading we see some *right* questions being asked. Questions which had the potential to lead the inquirers directly into the truth. Questions which would change their lives for eternity.

Right Question #1: "How can this be?" (Vs. 7)

What had the people observed that prompted this question?

Why is this a good question?

152 Finding Your Way

Right Question #2: "What does this mean?" (Vs. 12)

Who are they asking? (Vs. 12)

Who volunteers an answer? And what do they say? (Vs. 13)

The world always seeks to minimize God's work. Can you think of any ways that people explain away God's work today?

Who else volunteers an answer to the question, "What can this mean?" (vs. 14)

Remember, this is Peter - who was previously afraid to speak up about Jesus in public. In fact, at the very time of Jesus' greatest need, Peter pretended to not even know who He was.

Two life-changing events brought Peter to this point of boldness in Acts 2

John 21:1-14   What did Peter discover for himself?

Acts 2:1-4   What did Peter receive?

Peter believed the resurrection of Jesus was true and received the Holy Spirit. He was thereby empowered to carry out the great assignment which Jesus gave them right before he exited from the earth. The great assignment was this: "Tell people about me everywhere" (Acts 1:8).

Here Peter steps forward and speaks up, instead of shrinking back or running away. He has gone from *wondering* to *witnessing*!

Whose prophesies does Peter point to in his sermon?

Acts 2:17-21   Prophecy of _____
Summary:

Acts 2:25-35   Prophecy of _____
Summary:

GOD

INTERTESTAMENTAL PERIOD
400 YEARS
GREEK LANGUAGE
SYNAGOGUES
PEACE
ROADS

ZECHARIAH & ELIZABETH
JOHN THE BAPTIST
MARY & JOSEPH

JESUS' BIRTH
JESUS' BAPTISM
JESUS' TEMPTATION
SERMON ON THE MOUNT
JESUS' MIRACLES
INCLUDING:
FEEDING 5,000
HEALING BLIND MAN
JESUS' TRIAL BEFORE PILATE
JESUS' CRUCIFICTION
JESUS' RESURRECTION
JESUS APPEARS FOR 40 DAYS
JESUS' ASCENSION

Kingdom of God PRESENT

60. HOLY SPIRIT COMES INTO BELIEVERS

61. CHURCH BEGINS

Kingdom of God PROCLAIMED

Lesson Forty

What important conclusion does Peter want his listeners to face? (vs. 36)

Why is this the central issue?

Right Question #3: "What should we do?" (Vs. 37)

How did Peter answer this question in verse 38?

PRAYER MOMENT

"How can this be?"
"What can this mean?"
"What should we do?"

It is a thrill when someone asks us the perfect question! Maybe you can think of a time when you have experienced this. I'll never forget when my sister-in-law, who doesn't yet know Jesus, said to me, "Can someone just tell me what God is doing?" In that moment, God made it clear that this was an opportunity to share His plan of salvation with her. She didn't accept Jesus that day, but I know the Lord can use that conversation, along with many others, to bring her to Himself one day.

Who do you wish would ask you a "*right* question?" _____

What do you wish they would ask?

Even more difficult: how would *you* answer?

Spend some time praying that this person would start asking the *right questions*, and that the Holy Spirit would equip you, as He did Peter, with the right answer.

☐ *Check here when you have filled out your timeline with the new entries from this lesson.*

Lesson Forty

BIBLICAL THEME:
THE KINGDOM OF GOD

God's _____

in God's _____

under God's _____

enjoying God's _____

In Acts chapter two we watched as God sent His Holy Spirit to inhabit the believers on the day of Pentecost. This marks another transition in our **KINGDOM OF GOD** theme. We called our previous phase of history (during which Jesus walked the earth and lived among the people) the Kingdom of God _____.

What was the final promise Jesus made to his disciples right before he returned to heaven? (Luke 24:49)

As we turn the page in our Bible, Jesus has returned to heaven. He then sent the Holy Spirit so His people could accomplish the calling He placed on their lives – the mission to demonstrate Jesus to the world and to make Him known. As Jesus-followers we remain here on earth to **proclaim** Him to the world. This period of God's work we will call "the Kingdom of God Proclaimed" and it is the period of time we are still in today.

God's PEOPLE: Who are God's people here?

God's PLACE: Are the people in the place where God intended them to be?

God's RULE: How are they doing following the lead of the Lord, their true King? Are they obeying Him?

God's BLESSING: Are the people enjoying God's blessing? How do we see that?

☐ *Check here when you have written "Kingdom of God Proclaimed" in Oval G on your Timeline.*

LESSON FORTY-ONE

PRAYER MOMENT

"Church." What does that word bring to your mind? Jot some thoughts below.

Now pray that today's lesson will broaden your understanding of what church is.

BIBLE PASSAGE

Read Acts 2:42-47 and use the space below to record any questions it brings to mind or things you notice.

Reaching back into my childhood memories, I can hear the echo of my small footsteps on the gleaming slate floor. It was not often I was in this massive space alone, but that day I was. The stained-glass windows cast glittering light-filled patterns on the floor as the soothing sun shone in. High above, the ceiling was trimmed with heavy wooden beams which held up its peak. Pews worn soft with time lined the cross-shaped space. The regal lectern at the front of the room stood on the crimson carpet, ready and waiting for the next service to begin. Without the organ playing that day, it was a quiet room, but it was filled with music and memories for me. It was a place where I began to understand the wonder and majesty of God. To me, this was church.

What childhood memories do you have of church?

The word "church" often calls to mind an image of a building. Perhaps that was the case for you. But do you realize that when the church began there were no buildings? At the inception of the church, the activities that occupied the Christians were what distinguished them. Today, their example displays for us the function of the church in its truest sense. Let's look at these beginning stages to witness what Jesus had established then, and how He intends to continue that today.

During the 40 days between Jesus' resurrection and ascension He gave His disciples this assignment:

"Go and make disciples of all the nations, baptizing them in the name of the Father and the Son and the Holy Spirit. Teach these new disciples to obey all the commands I have given you. And be sure of this: I am with you always, even to the end of the age."
Matthew 28:19-20

Underline the things the disciples were instructed to do in these verses.

This instruction is known as "The Great Commission." Paraphrase what that title is meant to convey:

The Great Commission = _____

They were to begin there in Jerusalem, and then radiate out to the surrounding areas, bringing the amazing story of Jesus to "all nations." Consider how expansive this assignment was.

How would this fledgling group of new believers ever accomplish such a massive task? What would they need to succeed?

These believers would have to continue growing in their understanding of God and they would need to grow to support one another.

It's during this time that these believers began to be known as "Christians," which literally meant "little Christs." And as these Christians went out and made disciples, they also brought new believers into their fellowship. This was the start of the church! In some ways it looked different than today, but in many ways it was the same.

Again, read Acts 2:42-47 and list all the things which occupied and characterized these early Christians.

This is the pattern for the church! It is essential that you find a lot of commonalities between the activities of the early believers and the activities of the church where you worship.

Which of these same marks can be found in your own church? (Rate your church on a scale of 1-10 in these areas.)

Do you see your church devoted to **teaching of the Bible**?.................1 2 3 4 5 6 7 8 9 10

Is there healthy **fellowship** among the people? 1 2 3 4 5 6 7 8 9 10

Are people devoted to **prayer**, both at church and on their own?.......1 2 3 4 5 6 7 8 9 10

Is there a sense of **awe** and **wonder** at how God is at work?................1 2 3 4 5 6 7 8 9 10

Do the people of the church **care for each other** in practical ways?..................1 2 3 4 5 6 7 8 9 10

Is there a **concern for the poor**? Does the church work to meet their needs?...1 2 3 4 5 6 7 8 9 10

Is there an emphasis on **worshipping** God?...1 2 3 4 5 6 7 8 9 10

Is the **Lord's Supper** practiced with the message of the **gospel** it represents?.1 2 3 4 5 6 7 8 9 10

Are **new believers** being added to your church fellowship?................1 2 3 4 5 6 7 8 9 10

GOD

INTERTESTAMENTAL PERIOD
400 YEARS
GREEK LANGUAGE
SYNAGOGUES
PEACE
ROADS

ZECHARIAH & ELIZABETH
JOHN THE BAPTIST
MARY & JOSEPH

JESUS' BIRTH
JESUS' BAPTISM
JESUS' TEMPTATION
SERMON ON THE MOUNT
JESUS' MIRACLES
INCLUDING:
FEEDING 5,000
HEALING BLIND MAN
JESUS' TRIAL BEFORE PILATE
JESUS' CRUCIFICTION
JESUS' RESURRECTION
JESUS APPEARS FOR 40 DAYS
JESUS' ASCENSION

HOLY SPIRIT COMES INTO BELIEVERS
CHURCH BEGINS

Kingdom of God PRESENT

Kingdom of God PROCLAIMED

63. CHURCH AGE

Lesson Forty-One

As you reflect on these attributes, perhaps you notice some that are being done in your church, but you are not experiencing personally. How would you evaluate yourself in these areas? (Rate yourself on a scale of 1-10.)

Are you putting effort into learning from your church's **Bible teaching**?............................1 2 3 4 5 6 7 8 9 10

Have you invested in cultivating healthy **fellowship** for yourself at church?....................1 2 3 4 5 6 7 8 9 10

Are you devoted to **prayer**, both at church and on your own?..1 2 3 4 5 6 7 8 9 10

Do you have a sense of **awe** and **wonder** at how God is at work?.....................................1 2 3 4 5 6 7 8 9 10

Do you **care for others at church** in practical ways?..1 2 3 4 5 6 7 8 9 10

Do you have a **concern for the poor** and work to meet needs?...1 2 3 4 5 6 7 8 9 10

Are you entering into **worshipping** God both at church and on your own?....................1 2 3 4 5 6 7 8 9 10

Are you leaning into the celebration of the **Lord's Supper** at church?............................1 2 3 4 5 6 7 8 9 10

Are you **inviting friends** to come to church so they can hear about Jesus?...................1 2 3 4 5 6 7 8 9 10

Choose one attribute of the church which you would like to participate in or experience more.

Write it here: _____

How might you go about doing that?

PRAYER MOMENT

Close your study today in prayer, talking with God about your desire to enter into this aspect of the church to a greater degree. As you pray, listen to any insight He might give you about this. Write anything that comes to mind here.

☐ *Check here when you have filled out your timeline with the new entries from this lesson.*

LESSON FORTY-TWO

PRAYER MOMENT

What are some needs around you that you have noticed in recent days? Pray about each one as you list them below.

BIBLE PASSAGE

Read Acts 3:1-11 and use the space below to record any questions it brings to mind or things you notice.

List the main characters in this story.

Next to the names write what you know about each of them as the story opens. (Use the details in verse 2 to provide a description of the man.)

Draw a sketch of this crippled beggar.

In your drawing above,
- Label the need which Peter and John heard about from the man in vs. 3 **"The Need"**
- Label the need which Peter and John wanted to address in vs. 6 **"The Need Beyond the Need"**

Kingdom of God Proclaimed 159

Lesson Forty-Two

The Need – this is what the man was readily aware of. It was immediate and on the surface, an "in-your-face" need. He was asking for help with this need.

However, beyond this was a deeper need, **The Need Beyond the Need.** Perhaps he had resigned himself to this. He didn't know if even God could help him here, so why bother hoping that things could ever be different? Remember, he had been "lame from birth," verse 2 says. How could this not be a permanent condition? It was all he had ever known.

Peter says in verse 6, "I'll give you what I have." What was it he wanted to give the beggar?

Continue reading in this passage to understand what went on beneath the surface in this man's healing (vs. 12-16). What had happened within the man?

Understand that "the name of Jesus Christ" is more than just letters and syllables. In the Bible "name" represents the totality of who a person is: his character, his authority, his abilities, his whole being.

With this in mind, why was the name of Jesus Christ what the beggar needed?

What if Peter had just said "get up and walk"? How does Jesus' name matter?

Previously unaware of the power of Jesus' name, this poverty-stricken, handicapped man was now healed. Even more importantly, he experienced an encounter with Jesus.

Verse 7 explains that "the man's feet and ankles were instantly _____ and _____."

In the parenthesis write some synonyms for those words: (   )   (   )

What do you imagine this man's life was like after this event? (Look for hints in verses 8-11.)

As this scene closes in verse 11 we see the healed man holding tightly to Peter and John. And don't you imagine that from them this man learned to hold tightly to Jesus? After all, that was his **deepest need**.

160 Finding Your Way

PRAYER MOMENT

Draw a sketch of yourself, indicating a need in your life, and label that "**The Need**."

Is it possible that sometimes in our lives we are focused only on the need at the surface, when God wants to use this to drive us to face a deeper need? A place where we need more of Him?

Consider your need above. What may be a deeper need which the Lord wants you to face? A need where Jesus Christ can meet you. Lay this before the Lord in prayer below.

We need an encounter with Jesus' name to do the deeper work.
We need an understanding of who He is,
and the application of His healing power to this situation
for accomplishing lasting change.

LESSON FORTY-THREE

PRAYER MOMENT

Pray through the lyrics below.

> "The pages of history, they tell me it's true
> That it's never the perfect, it's always the ones with the scars that You use.
> It's the rebels and the prodigals.
> It's the humble and the weak.
> The misfit heroes You choose tell me there's hope for sinners like me."

"Broken Things," Matthew West, 2017

paradigm shift (n): 1. a fundamental change in approach or underlying assumptions 2. a fundamental change in an individual's view of how things work in the world 3. a time when the usual and accepted way of doing or thinking about something changes completely

Can you think of an example of a change you have witnessed which was so dramatic that it could be called a "paradigm shift?"

The Scripture reading before us today features a **spiritual paradigm shift**. Keep an eye out for the utter transformation of one man who experienced a fundamental change in his assumptions and his view of how things work in the world. You'll see how this rippled out and altered his entire life focus.

BIBLE PASSAGE

Read Acts 9:1-31 and use the space below to record any questions it brings to mind or things you notice.

SAUL BEFORE

Purpose: What was Saul's life all about? What was his purpose / mission (Vs. 1-2)?

KEY QUESTION

What was the key question Saul needed to have answered (Vs. 5)?

What was the answer (Vs. 5)?

Why did this answer hold significance?

HOW THE GOOD NEWS ABOUT JESUS WAS CONVEYED TO SAUL

Who did God give this assignment to (Vs. 10-12)?

How did this man initially feel about this calling (Vs. 13-14)?

Explain how these two differed:
Who Ananias perceived Saul to be (Vs. 13-14)   Who God perceived Saul to be (Vs. 15)

How did Ananias finally carry out this assignment (Vs. 17-18)?

How did Saul respond (Vs. 18-20)?

SAUL AFTER

Purpose: What was Saul's mission now? Look for key phrases that tell you what his unique ministry was (Vs. 22-30).

In what way did the answer to his "key question" become part of his own gospel presentation (Vs. 20)?

What was the ripple effect of Saul's conversion (Vs. 31)?

Lesson Forty-Three

Have you experienced a **spiritual paradigm shift** like Saul did? A time when you were faced with the need to alter your assumptions about how you relate to God, and to therefore adjust what your life is all about? Take a few minutes to explore how this process has unfolded for you. (You may not be able to fill in all of the following, depending on where you are in your journey, but fill in whatever you can.)

YOU BEFORE

Purpose: What was your life all about before you came to know Jesus? What was your focus, your "mission?"

KEY QUESTION

What was the key question about God which you needed to have answered?

What was the answer?

Why did this answer hold significance?

HOW THE GOOD NEWS ABOUT JESUS WAS CONVEYED TO YOU

How did you hear about Jesus? There may have been multiple times you heard the "gospel" (the good news about Jesus). Jot down all you remember.

Explain how these two differed:
Who you knew yourself to be   Who God saw you *could* be

Was there a person like Ananias in your life who shared the gospel with you in a way you could finally understand? If so, what did they say?

How did you respond to the gospel?

Finding Your Way

YOU AFTER

Purpose: What do you believe your mission is now? (Be specific)

In what way could the answer to your "key question" become part of your own gospel presentation?

What has been the ripple effect of your conversion?

What you have outlined on these two pages is your own "testimony" - the story of your spiritual journey. Realize that your simple story is powerful! Just as you and I gain inspiration and encouragement from reading the account of how Saul came to Christ, your story can challenge others.

Now that you've given your testimony some thought, look for a chance to share it with someone. It can be impactful to talk about the **key question** which you needed to have answered, **and how learning that answer changed your life**. It's all about a spiritual paradigm shift!

As you read further in the New Testament, you will see that Saul's name was changed to Paul. (Yes! This is the Apostle Paul!) His name change is a demonstration of what he would later write about in II Corinthians 5:17: '...Anyone who belongs to Christ has become a new person. The old life is gone; a new life has begun! Paul's Christianity meant a radical change in his whole nature.

Paul's Spiritual Paradigm Shift

Saul wanted believers to suffer (Vs.1-2)	Saul learned he must suffer for Christ (Vs. 16)
Saul was blinded (Vs. 8)	Saul then saw a vision (Vs. 12)
Saul wanted to get his hands on believers to kill them (Vs. 1-2)	Ananias laid hands on Saul and healed him (Vs. 17)
Saul balked at the faith	Saul was baptized into the faith (Vs. 18)
Saul wanted to kill Jews who converted (Vs. 1-3)	Saul wanted to convince Jews to convert (Vs. 20)
Saul tried to extinguish the church (Vs. 1-2)	Saul worked to expand the church (Vs. 31)

PRAYER MOMENT

Paul's Christianity transformed him; does yours transform you? Spend some time in prayer contemplating that question.

☐ *Check here when you have filled out your timeline with the new entries from this lesson.*

Timeline:

GOD

INTERTESTAMENTAL PERIOD
400 YEARS
GREEK LANGUAGE
SYNAGOGUES
PEACE
ROADS

ZECHARIAH & ELIZABETH
JOHN THE BAPTIST
MARY & JOSEPH

JESUS' BIRTH
JESUS' BAPTISM
JESUS' TEMPTATION
SERMON ON THE MOUNT
JESUS' MIRACLES
INCLUDING:
FEEDING 5,000
HEALING BLIND MAN
JESUS' TRIAL BEFORE PILATE
JESUS' CRUCIFICTION
JESUS' RESURRECTION
JESUS APPEARS FOR 40 DAYS
JESUS' ASCENSION

Kingdom of God PRESENT

HOLY SPIRIT COMES INTO BELIEVERS
CHURCH BEGINS

62. SAUL PAUL

Kingdom of God PROCLAIMED

CHURCH AGE

LESSON FORTY-FOUR

PRAYER MOMENT

"Your eternal word, O LORD, stands firm in heaven. Your faithfulness extends to every generation, as enduring as the earth you created."
Psalm 119:89-90

Thank the Lord for His faithfulness and the truth of His Word as you open your Bible today.

BIBLE PASSAGE

Read Acts 10:1-48 and use the space below to record any questions it brings to mind or things you notice.

Can you think of any prejudices that you or your relatives have struggled with? What, specifically, was the message you or they were erroneously believing?

In today's passage, we get a unique glimpse into the mysterious work of God in two places at the same time. Two people would have to change their assumptions in order for their lives to intersect, and for God's plan to unfold. Look through the keyhole and see what God was doing in the lives of these two individuals...

Acts 10:1-8

Who?

What details are given about him?

What did God tell this man?

How did God get his message to him?

Acts 10:9-20

Who?

What details are given about him?

What did God tell this man?

How did God get his message to him?
Draw the vision he saw and write the explanation under it.

You see, Cornelius was someone too different, too unlike these Jewish believers. They simply couldn't imagine that he could ever be a Christian like them. He was part of the Roman army which occupied their land, for heaven's sake! A Gentile! Impure and unclean! How could *their* faith be for someone like *him*?!

But God had an **ESSENTIAL TRUTH** to convey to Peter in verse 15:

"Do not call something _____ if God has made it _____."

Did Peter get it? What does Peter say in the following verses which shows his presuppositions were being corrected?

Vs. 26

Vs. 28

Vs. 34

Vs. 43

Who do you imagine to be outside the reach of the gospel, and why?

Realize that God is at work in the life of this person at this very moment, stirring things up. He is allowing life to disappoint and fail them so that they will look for more. So that they will look to Him. Just as Peter had no idea that God was churning things up in Cornelius' heart, so you may not be able to see what He is doing in the life of your friend. But be assured, He is at work!

Outline below the key points in Peter's explanation of the Gospel as he presents it to Cornelius in Vs. 36-43.

Lesson Forty-Four

Now write your own succinct gospel presentation, including what you feel is essential.

PRAYER MOMENT

Pray now that the Lord would be working in the lives of those you know who appear to be beyond His reach, loosening the soil in their lives, readying it for the seed of the gospel. Write their names below as you pray for them.

"… EVERYONE who believes in Him will have their sins forgiven through His name." Acts 10:43

LESSON FORTY-FIVE

PRAYER MOMENT

Pray through this verse, personalizing it as you do.

"And this is my prayer: that your love may abound more and more in knowledge and depth of insight, so that you may discern what is best…"
Philippians 1:9-10a)

How would our world define the word "love?"

BIBLE PASSAGE

Read I Corinthians 13:1-13 and use the space below to record any questions it brings to mind or things you notice.

As we might expect, the Lord defines love differently than our world does. Maybe you have heard this passage read during a wedding ceremony. Today, let's delve into how the Lord sees this most important topic.

This chapter opens with three "If I …" statements in verses 1-3. Below sum them up as math equations:

If I…	minus LOVE	= noisy gong / clanging cymbal
If I…	minus LOVE	=
If I…	minus LOVE	=

Kingdom of God Proclaimed 169

Lesson Forty-Five

Listed on the previous page in these "If I" statements are many admirable abilities and feats. These represent some of what would have been viewed as great accomplishments by the original readers of this letter. Bring this into today by listing here what qualities or achievements our contemporary culture esteems the most.

If I...	minus LOVE	=

The truths you listed from I Corinthians 13 are **God's equations – how it all adds up in His estimation.** All the great things man can do amount to nothing if love is absent. Love *adds value* to man's activities.

Since this is so, we need a firm grasp on what this love looks like.

LOVE IS / DOES...	LOVE IS NOT / DOES NOT...
Vs. 4	
Vs. 4	
	Vs. 4
	Vs. 4
	Vs. 4
	Vs. 5
	Vs. 5
	Vs. 5
	Vs. 5
	Vs. 6
Vs. 6	
	Vs. 7
	Vs. 7
Vs. 7	
Vs. 7	

Now go back through this list you have created and write a synonym in parenthesis next to each word or phrase. For example: <u>patient</u> (willing to wait)

PRAYER MOMENT

In your own life, what things do you value and aim to do? What do you spend your time on? (Answers might include "being a friend, caring for my children, working at my profession," etc.) Write these below as an "If I" statement.

If I…   **minus LOVE   =**

Now fill in under the "LOVE" space with a summary of your paraphrase of the attributes from vs. 4-7 which you came up with. It might read something like "As I seek to do these things I need to be willing to wait, to be caring, to be gentle, etc."

What goes in that last space in the equation above? You already know. If you strive to do all the things you have listed but do them without the type of LOVE which God values, you have accomplished **nothing**.

Yes, that is sobering. But understand the flip side of this too: if you work at each of the things on your list, and infuse your work with LOVE, you have really done **something**!

Take some time now to talk this through with the Lord in prayer:
- Tell Him what you are trying to accomplish in life.
- Ask Him to produce this type of love in you as you do these things.

LESSON FORTY-SIX

PRAYER MOMENT

Dietrich Boenhoffer said, "When Christ calls a man, He bids him 'Come and die.'" Pray that today you would understand more clearly what that means.

BIBLE PASSAGE

Read Philippians 2:1-18 and use the space below to record any questions it brings to mind or things you notice.

Begin today by asking yourself the questions Paul opens with in verse 1 of this chapter. Have you experienced any of these this week? Jot down anything that comes to mind.

Is there any **encouragement** from belonging to Christ?

Is there any **comfort** from his love?

Is there any **fellowship** together in the Spirit?

Is your heart **tender** and **compassionate**?

As you read the list above try replacing the phrase "*Is* there…" with "*Since* there is…" Be reminded today that these are blessings we receive from being joined with Christ – benefits we can expect as Christians!

List the things Paul is urging his readers to do as a result of these blessings they have experienced (vs. 2-4).

How would you sum up this type of living in one word? _____

Now that doesn't come naturally! What *does* come naturally is looking out only for our own interests. The qualities Paul is talking of here, however, are supernatural works that the Holy Spirit accomplishes in us because of our union with Jesus.

Remember that these letters in the New Testament, which we call Epistles, are a blend of both theology and instruction on Christian Living. Sometimes theology can seem heady and distant, but here Paul is going to show us that it is actually practical and inspiring. In this chapter he sandwiches some profound theology between his teachings on Christian living. He is saying:

<u>**Be**</u> like this
<u>**See**</u> the example of Christ
<u>**Be**</u> like this

The theology in the middle of this chapter serves as a stirring illustration of the way Paul is calling people to live. It is not an easy call. For Jesus, it involved a series of downward steps...

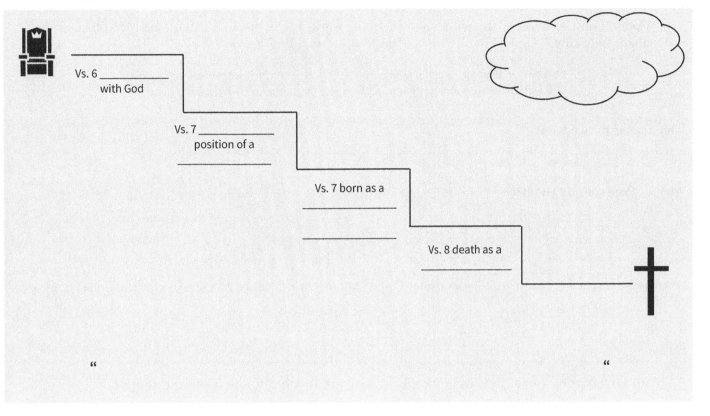

Vs. 6 _____ with God

Vs. 7 _____ position of a _____

Vs. 7 born as a _____

Vs. 8 death as a _____

Although this story is familiar, don't rush past it. Look at the progression above. Imagine what each step down meant for Jesus. What did He have to give up at each point? Write your thoughts next to each step above.

There was nothing pretty about this. Death on a cross was the most humiliating punishment of the time, so vile that it wasn't spoken about in proper society. Today, because of what it means for us, we venerate the cross, making it into church decor and jewelry we wear. And rightly so, because it is a symbol of freedom for us. But it was a symbol of humiliation and torture for Him, as an electric chair would be today. Nothing pretty about it.

And at this low point on the cross He cried out to His Father. What did He say? Read Mark 15:34 and write his words under the diagram above.

Not only did He suffer the humiliation of being publicly executed as a despicable criminal, and the pain of an excruciating death, but He experienced the torture of separation from His Father as well.

This is a path we would never willingly sign up for. But He did. Why?

However, for Jesus **it did not end there**. He was not defeated by the cross. Read verses 9-11 to understand what came **after the cross** for Jesus. Depict this information using the cloud in the diagram above. What was the final result of Jesus' sacrifice?

Kingdom of God Proclaimed 173

Lesson Forty-Six

**Jesus' story goes from a throne, to a cross, to a throne.
From glory to glory, with the cross in between.**

Coming on the heels of this summary of Jesus' work, in verses 12-13 there are two phrases about "working." Underline the words "work" and "working" below.

*"...Work hard to show the results of your salvation, obeying God with a deep reverence and fear.
For God is working in you, giving you the desire and the power to do what pleases Him."*

Who is doing the working?

What can you conclude from this?

List below the specific marks of this "working hard" and "working in" which are going on in a believer's life (vs. 14-16).

In the following verse circle the concepts of "you working hard" and "God working you."

"Let us run with endurance the race God has set before us. We do this by keeping our eyes on Jesus, the champion who initiates and perfects our faith. Because of the joy waiting him, he endured the cross, disregarding its shame. Now he is seated in the place of honor beside God's throne."
Heb. 12:1b-2

PRAYER MOMENT

In what relationship do you find it hard to exercise humility, setting aside your comforts and preferences and dignity to honor another person?

Write out a prayer below, remembering what you have discovered in Scripture today, and asking Jesus for help.

LESSON FORTY-SEVEN

> ## PRAYER MOMENT
>
> How do you picture God when you come to Him in prayer? Consider this as you begin in prayer. Ask Him to help you understand more through this study today.

Vacationing with my family recently, I observed a pattern I will not soon forget. My four-year-old grandson was having an amazing time in the pool – jumping in with a big splash, swimming without a life jacket, retrieving toys from the pool floor in the shallow end – he couldn't get enough of it. Seeing how much enjoyment the water gave him, I picked up a plastic baby pool from the local dollar store and set it on our balcony, but when I filled it he didn't have much interest in it. "Who wants that," he thought, "when I can play in the real pool!"

And so it is in our lives: what previously may have seemed pretty good becomes obsolete and out of date once we experience something that is immeasurably better.

Can you think of a time when you found this to be true?

In the passage before you today you're going to see how something that once seemed pretty good for God's people has been replaced with something that is far superior! Keep an eye out for the contrast as you read.

> ## BIBLE PASSAGE
>
> Read Hebrews 8:1-13 and use the space below to record any questions it brings to mind or things you notice.

This chapter of the Bible opens with a punchy statement. Transcribe the opening phrase of verse 1 here.

What do you think the writer of Hebrews is trying to convey by leading with this phrase?

As you continue reading in verse 1, who is the "main point" about? _____
Working our way through this study, you've seen He is the central character of the whole story of the Bible - He is the main point!

Kingdom of God Proclaimed 175

Jesus is of greatest importance because it was through Him that God established a new working relationship with mankind. This new working relationship (called a "covenant") had been prophesied in the Old Testament.

Summarize what these Old Testament prophecies foretold about the coming New Covenant.

Jeremiah 31:31-34   Ezekiel 36:25-27

So, in the Old Testament God related to mankind in one way, but in the New Testament, once Jesus entered into the story, God ushered in a New Covenant. To see why this new arrangement is immeasurably better, let's look at the contrast between the two. Write a few notes about each verse under its reference below.

	OLD COVENANT	**NEW COVENANT**
Priest	Hebrews 9:6-8	Hebrews 8:6
Sacrifices	Hebrews 10:1-4, 11	Hebrews 10:12
		Hebrews 9:12, 27-28
Tabernacle	Hebrews 8:5	Hebrews 8:2
	Hebrews 9:24-25	Hebrews 9:24-25
Access to God	Hebrews 9:6-10	Ezekiel 36:25-27

Mark 15 tells us it unfolded this way, *"The soldiers nailed Jesus to the cross...Then Jesus uttered another loud cry and breathed His last. And the curtain in the sanctuary of the Temple was torn in two, from top to bottom."*

Why was this curtain in the Temple ripped in half at the moment Jesus died on the cross?

Lesson Forty-Seven

What does that mean for you today?

Return now to Hebrews 8:1. Where did Jesus go when he left earth and what is His posture there?

After Jesus' death and resurrection, He left earth because He was done - He could sit down in heaven because His work was complete. In the Old Covenant, there was no chair for the priest in the temple. The high priests of the Old Testament worked ceaselessly day after day because their sacrifices were never able to fully eradicate the penalty of sin. These sacrifices were incomplete and temporary. But Jesus' sacrifice was complete and lasting.

Today, as you read this, Jesus is seated on His throne in heaven. What does this mean for you?

All other world religions say "do" - do these certain activities, prayers, and good works in hopes of accomplishing enough to make yourself acceptable to God. However, the good news in the Christian faith is summarized in the word "done." Jesus completed all that needed to be done to wipe away the sin which stood between you and God.

PRAYER MOMENT

How amazing is this: As a believer in Jesus, you personally have a High Priest who is seated today right beside God in heaven. There He sits, at the ready, waiting to present your requests to the Father. Take a moment to close your eyes and picture this.

Continuing to meditate on this image of your High Priest Jesus on His throne in heaven, spread out before Him the prayer requests you carry as a heavy burden today.

"Therefore, He is able to save completely those who come to God through Him,
because He always lives to interced for them."
Hebrews 7:25

Kingdom of God Proclaimed

LESSON FORTY-EIGHT

PRAYER MOMENT

"History is a story written by the finger of God."
C.S. Lewis

As you open your study today, praise God for His activity in human history.

Just yesterday my daughter asked me about my first date with her dad. "What? I haven't ever told you this before?" I said. Well, I had told her before, but she wanted to hear it again. So, my husband and I recounted our story to her, which began 31 years ago. It came so close to never happening, since the first time he asked me out I said "no." (It was comical to hear how different his take on that was than mine!) What fun it was to trace our story for our 15 year old, and to see God's hand in it once again.

There is something powerful about remembering our history. Somehow when we look back over a wide swath of time, the Lord's presence is more vivid. We see how all of the details fit together, and how one thing is dependent upon another. Miraculous!

There are a few chapters in God's word which do this same thing, tracing the story of the Israelites over a wide span of time. They are truly beautiful! As we read them, we see the lid of the puzzle box – the beautiful picture which all of the individual pieces make when they are put together. Today you will have the blessing of examining one of these chapters, Hebrews 11.

BIBLE PASSAGE

Read Hebrews 11:1-40 **aloud**, if possible, and use the space below to record any questions it brings to mind or things you notice.

As you read, notice that some of the characters referred to in this chapter are ones we studied together, while others are unfamiliar. Let's focus in on **just the people we have touched on throughout this study**.

NAMES OF WHO SHOWED FAITH:	WHAT THEY DID:
Vs. 3 By faith ____we____ ...	Understand the universe was made at God's command, out of nothing visible
Vs. 7 By faith _____ ...	
Vs. 8, 10 By faith _____ ...	

178 Finding Your Way

What did Abraham focus on to get through this uncertain time (Vs. 10)?

What were these people looking for (Vs. 13-16)?

Vs. 17-19 By faith _____ ...

Vs. 20   By faith _____ ...

Vs. 21   By faith _____ ...

Vs. 22   By faith _____ ...

Vs. 23-28 By faith _____ ...

What was he looking toward (Vs. 26)?

Who did he keep his eyes on (Vs. 27)?

Vs. 29-30 By faith _____ ...

Vs. 30-37 By faith ___various people___ ... (List just the verbs that indicate what they did.)

What did they place their hope in (Vs. 35)?

Now go back through your list above, starting with vs. 3, and circle the verbs, detailing what each of these people did.

(Ex: By faith we... (understand) the universe was made at God's command, out of nothing visible.)

Why was my daughter so interested in how her dad and I started dating? Maybe because, at 15, she is forming ideas about how she might meet her husband. *"What might this look like?" "How could it happen?"*

In the same way, we look at the Israelite's history and ask, *"What did it look like for these people to follow God?"* In studying them, we begin to understand what it might look like to live a God-ward life.

Lesson Forty-Eight

Compile a list of all the verbs you found...

By faith they...

Looking at your list, how would you characterize what they were able to do by faith?

Beyond what they were able to *do*, there was an **underlying mindset** which rings like a chorus throughout this chapter. We have marked this off in the boxes with borders on the previous pages.

Looking at all of these boxes, how would you summarize the focus which these individuals had?

All of this accomplished **by faith**! Then it's pretty important we understand what the word "faith" means. What do you think the word "faith" means when we read it in the Scripture?

PRAYER MOMENT

Imagine your life as a faith marathon. You have completed the first portion of the race and it lies *behind* you. As you reflect on this part which you have already finished, complete the statement below, focusing on the things you would not have made it through without the Lord's help:

By faith I...

Part two of the race lies *before* you. But realize you don't run in isolation. Read Hebrews 12:1. Surrounding you along the course are all those who have gone before: Noah, Abraham, Isaac, Jacob, Joseph, Moses, the Israelites, and others you have known personally who have gone before you to heaven. It's really quite a crowd! There they are, each cheering you on, chanting out what they've learned through their own strenuous races. As their voices of encouragement ring in your ears, in prayer, commit to what still lies before you in this race:

By faith I...

☐ **Write "You Are Here" next to the star on your timeline.**

LESSON FORTY-NINE

> ## PRAYER MOMENT
>
> *"Teach us to number our days, that we may gain a heart of wisdom."*
> Psalm 90:12
>
> Pray this for yourself as you begin your study today.

Leaving the restaurant after breakfast, the brochures on the wooden display catch your eye: "Travel Back in Time at the Amish Village," "Explore the Secrets of the Indian Cavern," "Shop for Bargains at the Outlet Mall." You pick up a few and peruse them as you walk back to your car. "Maybe I'll make time to visit one of these places," you think as you settle into the driver's seat. But then you toss the brochures onto the seat next to you, and don't give them another thought even when you pick them up to throw them away a few days later. Truth is, none of them looked wonderful enough to change your plans. Some destinations are like that.

Others, however, really grip your attention. Perhaps a commercial for white sandy beaches warmed by golden sunrises replays in your memory long after it's over. Or maybe the vision of snowspray flying off of skis on a pine dotted mountain lingers in your thoughts. Possibly a gondola weaving through an Italian waterway, the sun sparkling on the ripples in the water, is a sight you yearn to witness in person. "Now that would be worth planning for," you think. "That is something to get excited about!"

What travel destination is on your bucket list? _____

"Where would I like to go before I kick the bucket?" we ask. But perhaps an even more gripping question is "Where will I go *when* I kick the bucket?" If you are a Christian you can be assured your future is in heaven. But perhaps heaven is some far-off, vague notion, that doesn't really have too much appeal.

How do you envision heaven?

Often we think of heaven as one long experience of the same thing. But as we read in the Bible, we find that there is a **heaven that is now** and a **heaven yet to come**. Right now, when a believer dies they go to the heavenly place we think of – celebrating the presence of God and Jesus, reunited with other believers who have died in times past. It is wonderful! But even more magnificent is the heaven that is yet to come. The book of Revelation talks of this. Since this is our eventual journey's end (our true "bucket list destination") let's examine this mysterious place.

Lesson Forty-Nine

BIBLE PASSAGE

Read Revelation 21:1-26, 22:1-6 and use the space below to record any questions it brings to mind or things you notice.

Let's approach our study of heaven remembering that this is a real and tangible travel destination for those who are in Christ. On this page, create a **tri-fold travel brochure** of what you find in today's reading. Focusing on some of the "**LANDMARKS**" and "**FEATURES**" of the New Jerusalem which you find most interesting, turn this page horizontally and make it into a travel brochure. Write (and maybe sketch?) what is described.

182 Finding Your Way

PRAYER MOMENT

In some ways, this passage is written in code language. How could John, the writer, describe something indescribable? By likening it to what we are familiar with.

Now for the challenging part: below, create **another tri-fold brochure that corresponds to the one you made** on the previous page, explaining as best you can the SYMBOLISM OF EACH LANDMARK you featured. Take some time in prayer to ponder WHAT THE LORD WANTS TO CONVEY through each feature and explain them in the pattern below.

GOD

INTERTESTAMENTAL PERIOD
400 YEARS
GREEK LANGUAGE
SYNAGOGUES
PEACE
ROADS

ZECHARIAH & ELIZABETH
JOHN THE BAPTIST
MARY & JOSEPH

JESUS' BIRTH
JESUS' BAPTISM
JESUS' TEMPTATION
SERMON ON THE MOUNT
JESUS' MIRACLES
INCLUDING:
FEEDING 5,000
HEALING BLIND MAN
JESUS' TRIAL BEFORE PILATE
JESUS' CRUCIFICTION
JESUS' RESURRECTION
JESUS APPEARS FOR 40 DAYS
JESUS' ASCENSION

Kingdom of God **PRESENT**

HOLY SPIRIT COMES INTO BELIEVERS
CHURCH BEGINS
SAUL/PAUL
CHURCH AGE

Kingdom of God **PROCLAIMED**

 YOU ARE HERE

181

KINGDOM OF GOD
PERFECTED

LESSON FIFTY

PRAYER MOMENT

Jesus invites us to come to Him, but some reject this invitation. Meditate on the following verses, and then pray about your response to His invitation.

Jesus said, "You search the Scriptures because you think they give you eternal life.
But the Scriptures point to me! Yet you refuse to come to me to receive this life…
I have come to you in my Father's name, and you have rejected me."
John 5:39, 43

"But to all who believed Him and accepted Him, He gave the right to become children of God."
John 1:12

Today we arrive at the very last section in the very last chapter of the Bible. God knew, when He had various authors write the books of the Bible, that this would be the final one in the arrangement. For well over a thousand years, when people have read the Bible they have ended with the reading of this section. There is a unique weightiness to this passage.

Knowing what you now know, having nearly completed this overview study of the Bible, what do you anticipate the subject of this final section will be? _____

What last thoughts do you imagine the Lord would want to leave us with as we complete our reading of His Word? Write a paragraph below, as if you are John penning these final words of the Bible.

BIBLE PASSAGE

Read Revelation 22:7-21 and use the space below to record any questions it brings to mind or things you notice.

Kingdom of God Perfected

Lesson Fifty

I asked you to guess above, but now, having read these verses, what (more precisely, who) is the subject of this final section? _____

This is our final opportunity to gaze into who Jesus is. Read through this section again, and list here the phrases which are used to describe Jesus (see verses 13, 16, 20).

_____ _____

_____ _____

_____ _____

Let's examine these descriptions of Jesus. As you read below, underline any pertinent phrases, and then summarize what you've learned in the space provided below.

"I am *the Alpha and the Omega*" – verse 13

> "Alpha and Omega are the first and last letters of the Greek alphabet. Among Jewish rabbis it was common to use the first and last letters of the Hebrew alphabet to denote the whole of anything, from beginning to end…These [words] are also clear indications of the eternal nature of the Godhead."
> *(gotquestions.org, "What does it mean that Jesus is the Alpha and the Omega?")*

> "Who has done such mighty deeds, summoning each new generation from the beginning of time? It is I, the LORD the First and the Last. I alone am He."
> Isaiah 41:4

> "…fixing our eyes on Jesus, the author and perfecter of our faith."
> Hebrews 12:2 NASB

I am "The Alpha and the Omega" means that Jesus is…

"I am *the First and the Last, the Beginning and the End*" – verse 13

> "In the beginning God created the heavens and the earth."
> Genesis 1:1

> "In the beginning the Word [Jesus] already existed. The Word was with God, and the Word was God. He existed in the beginning with God. God created everything through him, and nothing was created except through him. So the Word became human, and made his home among us. He was full of unfailing love and faithfulness. And we have seen his glory, the glory of the Father's one and only Son." John 1:1-3, 14

> "He existed before anything else, and he holds all creation together."
> Colossians 1:17

I am "The First and the Last, the Beginning and the End" means that Jesus is…

"I am *the Source of David and the Heir to his throne*" – verse 16

To understand this name, we will be referring back to Lesson 24 (pages 97-99) of our study. In this lesson we learned that there would be a "new shoot from and old root." Look over your notes there to remember what this prophecy in Isaiah 11 was about.

I am "The Source of David and the Heir to his throne" means that Jesus is...

"I am *the Bright Morning Star*" – verse 16

"The phrase 'the bright morning star' is a reference to the planet Venus. When it rises in the sky, the sun will follow very soon – sometimes within a matter of minutes. Christ's coming means that God's light is about to shine FOREVER on the universe, making all wrongs right, wiping away all tears… On a long dark night, the appearance of the morning star means daybreak is imminent."
(Jesus.org, Randy Alcorn, "Why is Jesus called the "Morning Star?")

I am "The Bright and Morning Star" means that Jesus is...

"He is *the Faithful Witness*" – verse 20

"A witness tells what he has seen or heard. A faithful witness is one whose testimony is reliable every time."
(Jesus.org, Ray Pritchard, "Jesus: The Faithful Witness?")

"No one has yet discovered the word Jesus ought to have said, none suggested the better word he might have said. No action of his has ever shocked our moral sense. None has fallen short of the ideal. He is full of surprises, but they are all the surprises of perfection."
John Watson

"Actually I was born and came into the world to testify to the truth. All who love the truth recognize that what I say is true."
John 18:37b

I am "The Faithful Witness" means that Jesus is...

GOD

INTERTESTAMENTAL PERIOD
400 YEARS
GREEK LANGUAGE
SYNAGOGUES
PEACE
ROADS

ZECHARIAH & ELIZABETH
JOHN THE BAPTIST
MARY & JOSEPH

JESUS' BIRTH
JESUS' BAPTISM
JESUS' TEMPTATION
SERMON ON THE MOUNT
JESUS' MIRACLES
INCLUDING:
FEEDING 5,000
HEALING BLIND MAN
JESUS' TRIAL BEFORE PILATE
JESUS' CRUCIFICTION
JESUS' RESURRECTION
JESUS APPEARS FOR 40 DAYS
JESUS' ASCENSION

HOLY SPIRIT COMES INTO BELIEVERS
CHURCH BEGINS
SAUL/PAUL
CHURCH AGE

Kingdom of God PRESENT
Kingdom of God PROCLAIMED

YOU ARE HERE

64. JESUS' RETURN

Kingdom of God PERFECTED

Lesson Fifty

> Repeatedly, this section emphasizes that Jesus is coming back! But when is He coming? What clues do these verses give? (Vs. 7, 10, 12, 20)

It is amazing to know that Jesus will one day return to the earth. But this message isn't just an announcement that *He* is coming, it is also an invitation for *us* to come.

"Let anyone who is thirsty come," Jesus says in verse 17.

The invitation stands before you: "**Come**." One day this invitation will be no longer available to you; but today it remains. Have you responded? It is not enough to simply know all the facts you have learned throughout this Bible study. You must respond by personally coming to Jesus. The following question is the most important one in all of this study:

Have <u>you</u> come to Jesus? ____ yes ____ no

Jesus invites you to come to Him, bringing all your flaws and brokenness and sin. The beauty in His invitation is that you do not need to clean yourself up before you come to Him. In fact, your brokenness is the very reason He reaches out to you. You see, sin separates you from God. Since God is holy, He is not able to draw near to you because of the load of sin which you carry. But He did not want this distance to remain, especially since this separation becomes permanent and eternal once you die. God sent His Son Jesus, who lived a perfect life and was then put to death on the cross, as a substitute for you. He experienced separation from God on your behalf, so you don't have to remain distanced from God.

One day, you will stand before God. You either show up holding all your sin in your arms, or you show up clean and empty handed because you have accepted Jesus' sacrifice and asked Him to take your sin from you.

Come to Him! Accept the sacrifice He made on your behalf.
He *came* to earth for you…and will *come* again one day and wants to bring you to heaven.

PRAYER MOMENT

Spend some time in prayer contemplating the question, *"Have you come to Jesus?"* *
In closing, read aloud these words of Jesus:

> Jesus replied, "I am the bread of life. Whoever comes to me will never be hungry again. Whoever believes in me will never be thirsty. But you haven't believed in me even though you have seen me. However, those the Father has given me will come to me, and I will never reject them. For I have come down from heaven to do the will of God who sent me, not to do my own will. And this is the will of God, that I should not lose even one of all those he has given me, but that I should raise them up at the last day. For it is my Father's will that all who see his Son and believe in him should have eternal life. I will raise them up at the last day."
> John 6:35-40

* If you are unsure of what it means to "come to Jesus," ask a Christian friend, your Bible study leader, or a pastor. This is too important a question not to know for certain that you have answered it.

☐ *Check here when you have filled out your timeline with the new entries from this lesson.*

Lesson Fifty

BIBLICAL THEME:
THE KINGDOM OF GOD

God's _____

in God's _____

under God's _____

enjoying God's _____

In the Garden of Eden we saw…	The Kingdom of God _____
But sin entered and so…	The Kingdom of God _____
However, God did not abandon His plan; He came to Abraham and announced…	The Kingdom of God _____
It was a bumpy road, but God's people eventually entered the Promised land. Here they experienced…	The Kingdom of God _____
Judges led the people for awhile, then Kings, and the kingdom divided into the north and south. It's not a pretty picture, so God appointed prophets to speak to the people, which makes this period…	The Kingdom of God _____
There was a period of silence between the OT and NT. Then finally God's solution to man's predicament came on the scene: Jesus was born, thus began…	The Kingdom of God _____
Jesus lived a perfect life, died as a sacrifice for man's sin, rose from the dead, and returned to heaven. What a story to tell! That's why this period is…	The Kingdom of God _____
In our last lesson, we saw what is yet to come in history: an amazing future for those who put their faith in Jesus. What was lost at the Fall will be restored, and believers will live in God's presence. Sounds perfect again, doesn't it? So we'll call this last phase…	The Kingdom of God _____

Think about all of the things which will be restored by God in this final chapter. List below the reasons you think we call this last phase "The Kingdom of God Perfected."

How does this reflect God's original plan, "the Kingdom of God Pattern", that we saw back in Genesis?

Remember the markers we have looked at throughout our study (God's people in God's place under God's rule enjoying God's blessing)? What will be going on with each of these in this perfected kingdom?

☐ *Check here when you have written "Kingdom of God Perfected" in Oval H on your Timeline.*

BONUS LESSON

PRAYER MOMENT

You have made it to the last day of our study! As you open in prayer today, praise the Lord for the perseverance He gave you to complete this, and ask Him to solidify what you have learned.

FINAL TIMELINE REVIEW

We are going to review today by walking through your timeline twice.

First, turn to your timeline and talk through the story *aloud*, beginning with the first point, and continuing to the last point which you just added. Realize this history is literally "His story" - the historical account of God's unfolding work across time. So, tell it as a cohesive story, explaining the transitions in the ***Kingdom of God*** as you go.

Have you found that there are some blanks on your timeline that you didn't fill in as you worked through this book? Go ahead and make any corrections necessary on your timeline by flipping back through your book to find what you missed. (Remember the timeline runs along the right hand side of the lessons that included new entries.)

Now you're ready to make this timeline into a tool you can use in the future. Since you're nearing the end of this study, you don't want to leave this valuable tool in a closed book on your shelf. You've spent too much time recording everything there to let it go to waste. So, cut it out of the book, and also cut each page down the middle dotted line. Then staple your timeline together to keep it in order, or hole punch and connect the pages with a binder ring. (If you want to make your timeline more durable, copy it onto cardstock paper.)

For your second run-through review, read over your timeline again. This time, boil down the whole story into the ***twelve points*** in the historical account which you feel are the ***most important to and influential on the story as a whole***. Below, write your abbreviated timeline (turn your page and write vertically between the arrows).

Finally, sum up the whole story of the Bible in one sentence.

Bonus Lesson

See how much you have learned? You did it! You made it all the way to the end of this study. It is my hope that the Bible no longer feels like a muddle of separate stories to you, like pieces of a puzzle strewn across a table. You now have the lid to the puzzle box! You have the big picture of the Bible and understand how the smaller pieces fit in. You are prepared for a lifetime of filling in the details, as you continue to study the Bible.

You will find that your timeline can serve as a tool for you in the years to come. Tuck it into the back of your Bible and use it as you study. Write on it, adding details as you learn. When your pastor preaches on a certain passage, pull out your timeline to understand where you are in the bigger picture. When you start a new Bible study, refer to your timeline to understand where that study picks up in the overall story. You are now prepared.

PRAYER MOMENT

As you close your study today, and close this book, it is fitting that we praise God for this amazing Word He has given us! Paraphrase these verses into your own words as you pray, committing yourself to Him.

"Your eternal Word, O Lord,

stands firm in heaven.

Your faithfulness extends to

every generation,

as enduring as the earth you created.

Your regulations remain true to this day,

for everything serves your plans.

If your instructions hadn't sustained me with joy,

I would have died in my misery.

I will never forget your commandments,

for by them you give me life.

Teach me your decrees, O Lord;

I will keep them to the end.

Give me understanding

and I will obey your instructions;

I will put them into practice with all my heart."

Psalm 119:89-93, 33-34

Kingdom of God Perfected

WHERE DO I GO FROM HERE?

**"All these months this book has told me what to study each day,
and now that I'm done, I don't know what to read!"**

Often when we get to the end of a Bible study we don't know what to do next. Fortunately, there is an answer for this! Having completed this overview of the Bible, a natural next step is to complete a more detailed reading plan. You can pretty easily find another reading plan by searching online. You have the framework in place and, with your timeline beside you, you are now ready to fill in more details.

Keep it simple! Grab a journal, and **answer one or two of these questions about each passage** as you read:

- What does this section **tell me about God**?
- What does this section **reveal about mankind…and about me**?
- Is there a **nugget of truth** to remember?
- Are there **repeated words** in this passage?
- Do I see any **vivid contrasts** in this section?
- Is there a **verse to copy** down?
- Can I **paraphrase a section** to understand it better?
- Am I drawn to **memorize a verse** from this section?
- Do I find a **verse to pray** through?
- Can I **list some points** I want to remember?
- As I read this am I **prompted to pray for someone**?
- How can I **apply to my life** what I have read? What do I need to **do**?

Give yourself the freedom to use your journal in various ways as you study. No two days have to be the same. Some days you may have a lot to write, some days very little. Don't worry – no one is going to look at this but you! Let this journal be a tool to help you, not a weight that burdens you.

FOLLOW UP

Reinforce what you have learned through *Finding Your Way* to solidify what you have experienced through this study. Reach out to us and we will provide you with a list of additional follow up resources you can use to add to your learning. Find us at findingyourwaybiblestudy.com.

CAN YOU HELP?

Thank you for reading and engaging with *Finding Your Way!*

I really appreciate all of your feedback, and I love hearing what you have to say. I need your input to make the next version of this book and my future books better.

Please leave me an honest review on Amazon letting me know what you thought of the book.

Thanks so much!
Kim Burch

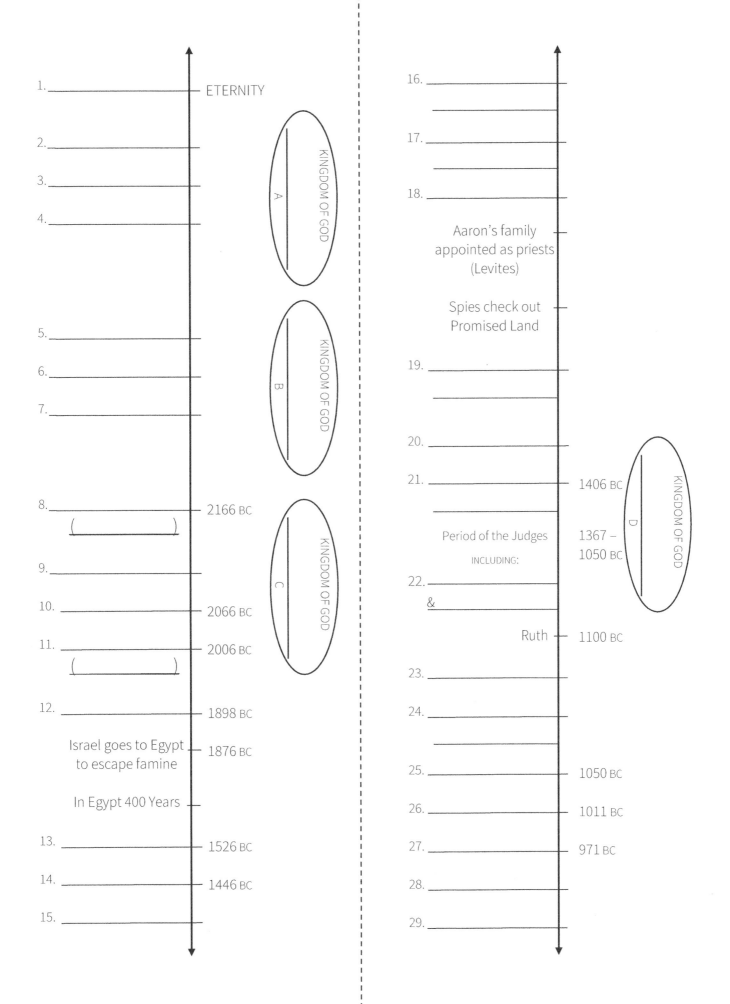

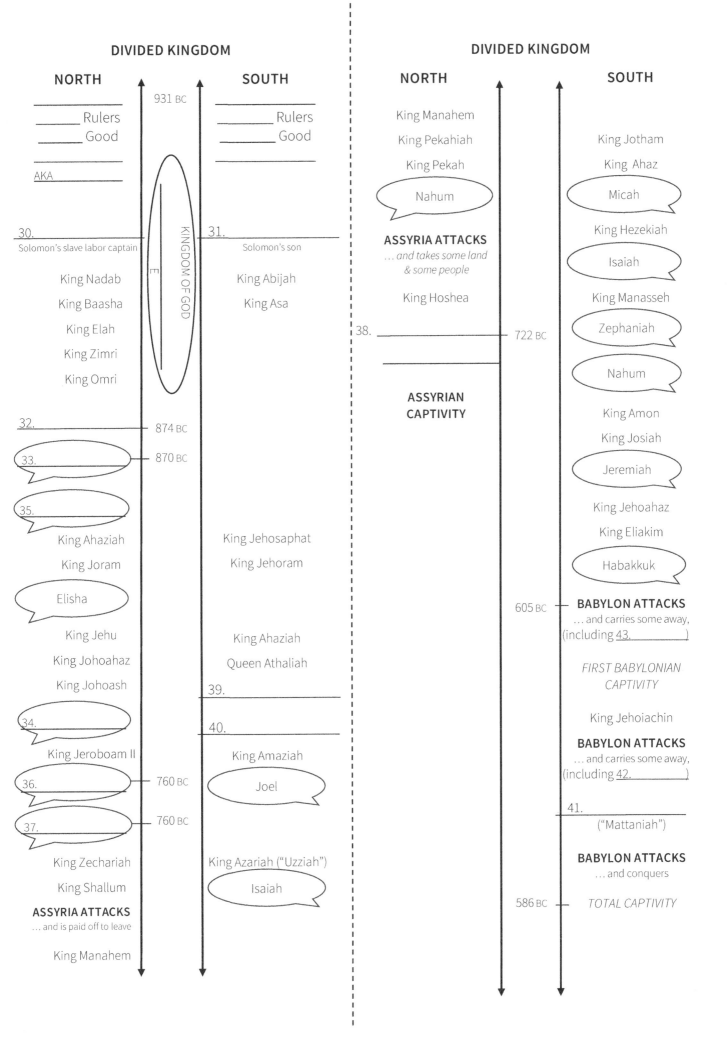

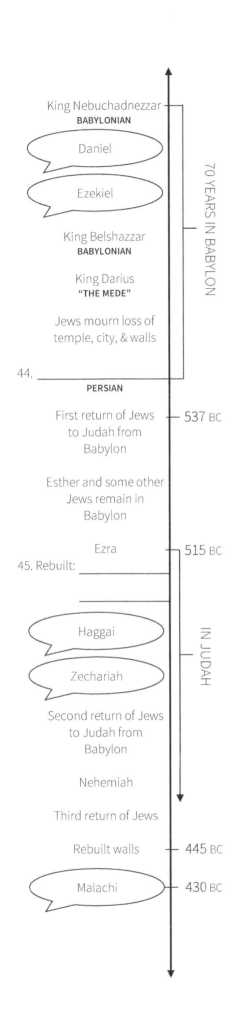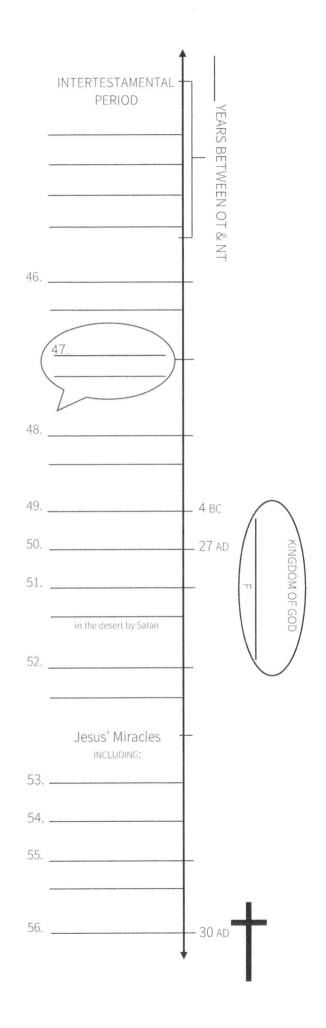

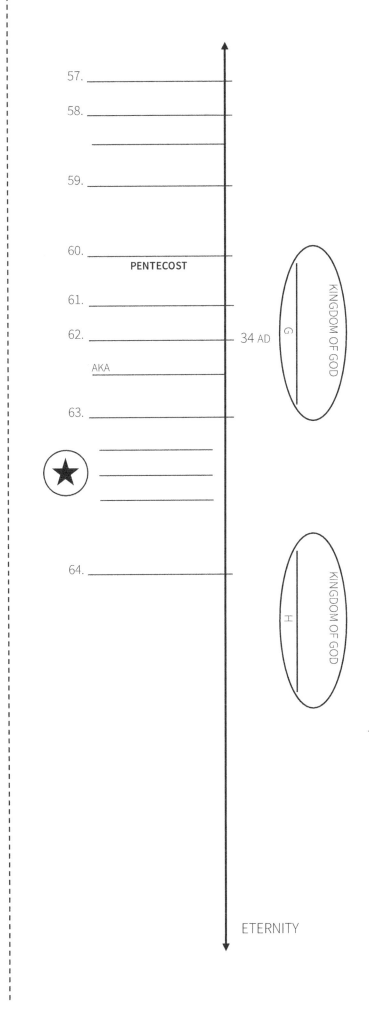

Made in United States
Orlando, FL
16 July 2025